# WARRIOR QUEEN

# WARRIOR QUEEN

SCOTT EDELMAN

BALLANTINE BOOKS • NEW YORK

A Ballantine Book
Published by The Ballantine Publishing Group
Copyright © 1999 by Scott Edelman

www.randomhouse.com/BB/

ISBN 0-345-44145-1

Manufactured in the United States of America

First Ballantine Books Edition: April 2000

10  9  8  7  6  5  4  3  2  1

# ACKNOWLEDGMENTS

Special thanks must go to the following core members of my own Federation, without whom this book could not possibly have been wrestled into reality:

Joe Varda, for being the "Stone Cold" Steve Austin to my own Mankind; Dr. Mike Lano, for his memories of the early days; Barry Malzberg, for showing that it was possible to do the impossible; Lee Edelman, for all those years wrestling in our parents' house; Jeff Eisenberg, Tom Miller, Al Ortega, and Sue Schneider for keeping things in focus; Trevor Vartanoff, for his photographic memory; Irene Vartanoff, who by putting up with me has proven herself to surely be the Tenth Wonder of the World; my grandfather Nathan Goldstein, the former Brooklyn bookie, who must have planted wrestling in my genes and is laughing in the great gambling den in the sky; Mark Hintz and Carl Gnam, for saying no and then saying yes. Finally, most of all, thanks must go to Joanie Laurer for having had the courage and perseverance to become Chyna.

# CONTENTS

# WARRIOR QUEEN

# CHAPTER 1

# A WOMAN'S PLACE IS IN THE RING

The Great Pyramids of Egypt. The Hanging Gardens of Babylon. The Statue of Zeus at Olympia. The Temple of Artemis at Ephesus. The Mausoleum at Halicarnassus. The towering Colossus at Rhodes. The Lighthouse of Alexandria.

These are the Seven Wonders of the World. For centuries they have been considered the ultimate symbols of humanity's greatest achievements, works that have inspired awe with their size, their beauty, and their poetry. The wonder of their construction is nothing short of miraculous. They are the pinnacles to which mankind aspires. Unfortunately for us, no one today has seen more than a single one of these wonders, because only the pyramids have survived to this dawning of a new millennium. The remaining six of these wonders of the world have been rubble for centuries, destroyed by wars, earthquakes, and the ravages of time.

It wasn't until 1946 that an Eighth Wonder of the World was introduced into the universe and deemed worthy enough to join the lonely pyramids. Andre Rousimoff was an unbelievable phenomenon of creation. At age seventeen, young Andre was already seven feet tall. When he eventually entered the ring at seven-four and weighing 520 pounds, he could not be stopped, more a force of nature than a mere man. He was an anomaly in the wrestling world, all other contenders dwarfed by his mere presence. P. T. Barnum would have loved him. There was only one name for such as he—Andre the Giant, the Eighth Wonder of the World. He was a *true* giant of the ring.

Where other wrestlers could only make pretense to the title, demanding with their mouths what they could not take with their muscles or talents, Andre was the only human who could lay claim to that phrase *literally*. He remained undefeated—as defined by wrestling's often-fluid rules—for two decades, until losing to that powerful icon of eighties wrestling, Hulk Hogan, at Wrestlemania III in 1987. In the ring Andre was not only an unstoppable force and an immovable object, but outside of the ring, in his private life, he was very much like Fezzek, the gentle character whom movie fans will recall him playing in the 1987 fairy-tale film *The Princess Bride*. The medical world would say that he suffered from giantism, but at least he did manage in the three-ring circus of wrestling to find a life where he did not suffer. He simply grew until he could no longer, and then died peacefully in 1993, having remade the wrestling world.

And there the tally of the world's wonders stood frozen until a new contender approached the squared circle to demand the respect of all comers.

Joanie Laurer strides the packed arenas that are her workplace with supreme confidence. At five feet nine inches tall and weighing 201 pounds, this muscled black-clad grappler tosses the other wrestlers about like limp rag dolls. Dressed in a leather two-piece and sneering like Xena with an attitude, she marched uninvited into the wrestling world and remade it in her own captivating image—and she didn't need an antique sword to do it. Her impact was explosive, catapulting her to heights that it would have taken others far longer to attain.

She is undoubtedly the greatest woman wrestler of her age, perhaps even of all time. And by her confident smile, we know that she knows it. Perhaps she is even the greatest wrestler of *any* gender; the jury is still out on that one. But waiting for the verdict is one of the greatest spectacles of our age.

She has captivated audiences, commanded respect, and ridden the waves of popularity as no woman wrestler before her has. Her legions of fans are not just the traditional hard-core audience. She has reached beyond them to capture the nation's attention. A world watches in awe. Her chiseled features have stared back at us from the covers of *Newsweek* and *TV Guide*. Her sinews were more than sufficient to bend the mostly masculine WWF to her will. China, the continent, is large, but Chyna, the woman wrestling creation with raven hair and tight leather, is larger than life, a comic-book superhero made three-dimensional.

For she is no ordinary wrestler. She is Chyna, the Ninth Wonder of the World.

Her accomplishments are many, far greater than those of any other woman who has ever invaded this man's world. She was considered a tough enough battler to be drafted as one of the three founding members of the hell-raising D-Generation-X, alongside Shawn Michaels and Triple H. In January 1999 she became the first and only woman to have ever competed in the organized mayhem that is the Royal Rumble. She is the only woman to have ever worn the Intercontinental Championship Belt.

Chyna is the only woman worthy enough in the eyes of the fans and the wrestling press to be given serious consideration as a contender for a potential World Wrestling Federation Heavyweight Championship Belt. That match will come some-day—have no doubts about it. She has made it plain that she will not stand idly by while the mus-clebound men who think themselves her peers trade that trophy among themselves; she intends to someday reach out and seize it for herself. And once she has it, she will not let it go easily, or per-haps at all.

She is such a towering figure within the wrestling world that the other federations that must go head-to-head with the WWF feel they must compete not just with the reigning federa-tion, but with her personally. This can be seen by the fact that the masterminds at World Championship Wrestling made the mistake of failing to hire her when she came knocking that they responded to Chyna's astonishing success by coming up with their own wrestler called . . . Asia. Perhaps the WCW hoped to fool you with a name so close to Joanie's chosen nom de plume, but instead, all it reminds us of is that there are no substitutions for the woman called Chyna.

Joanie Laurer has made Chyna into probably one of the most recognizable female athletes in the world, and this warrior princess stands ready to conquer.

Chyna's magnetic ring personality has contributed in large part to the success of the World Wrestling Federation, which, now that it has gone public, has achieved a net worth of over one billion dollars, with 83 percent of that stock owned personally by Vince McMahon and his family. Wrestling has become a bigger business than ever before, with sales of over $340 million expected once the books are closed on 2000. Without the character of Chyna that Joanie Laurer has created and embodied, it is doubtful that so much would have been realized. Wrestling is bigger and better than ever, and Joanie Laurer is one of the core figures who has made it so. In the area of public acceptance of what was once considered only a lowbrow circus, Joanie Laurer is one of the best ambassadors the sport has ever had.

Strangely enough, once you learn her statistics, you realize that on the field of battle she seems far larger than the numbers that describe her dimensions would imply. Those cold, dry facts of height and weight are deceiving, perhaps because of our prejudicial preconceptions about the acceptable size of women. We look at her dwarfing the male wrestlers with her presence, men whom we already know from experience to themselves be imposing figures who could crush us ordinary citizens with an idle gesture, and assume that she surely must tip the scales and stretch the tape measures even farther than that. She has gone where no woman wrestler has ever gone before, and her cool stage presence makes us wish to know more of the mystery behind the character. Her size and strength are even more daunting to her opponents, whether male or female, than they are entertaining to the fans.

She has fought hard for her fabulous success, and she has had to fight hard, because no one was willing to hand it to her. She carved a path that did not exist before she decided to blaze it. Wrestling legend Lillian Ellison, who as the incomparable Fabulous Moolah dominated the women's wrestling scene for over twenty-eight years (and who is still making regular appearances as crowd pleaser and a major player in WWF events) gave Joanie Laurer her first break in the business, and after all these years is still one of her closest coworkers. Of Chyna and the woman who stands behind her, Ellison has proudly said, "When you talk about the type of lady performer to help lead the business into the year 2000, Chyna is at the forefront."

In fact, Chyna so dominates the sport, that when *Rampage* magazine polled its readers on their top choice for toughest female wrestler, she so dominated the category that she garnered just over eighty percent of the vote. The rest of her competition for the top spot in that poll was so slight that no other woman wrestler even got over five percent. And that tightly held monopoly on the public's regard seems unlikely to change anytime soon.

Who is Joanie Laurer, the brash young woman who transformed herself into a leather-clad wrestling superstar and leading force as the sport enters a new century?

Those who know her only from the forceful personality and actions of her cherished ring creation would be surprised to discover what a playful personality she demonstrates when backstage. She is a fairly complex woman as well, though; as with many of the most successful wrestlers, she has simplified her public persona. The more popular wrestlers in the industry have always been the ones most easily understood by an audience. Fans must be able to quickly grasp motivations and characters, and even as their idols act in a larger-than-life manner, must perceive that there is a resonance between performer and role, that even though they are not exactly alike, there is a connection of soul and spirit. And by embodying the high-concept wrestling role of a tough broad who wants to show up the big boys in an overwhelmingly male profession, Chyna has taken a stand for all women. By showing that a woman can compete on an equal footing, and believe in herself while doing so, she has taken a stand for women everywhere seeking to move into predominantly male career paths. In fact, she has taken a stand for all people of either gender who wish to crack open the doors and gain entrance to those places where they may be unwanted. Everybody loves this kind of underdog story, and amazingly, Chyna has even been able to retain the public's sympathy even when her storylines have turned her into a winner.

This tough but still surprisingly feminine woman has faced down the cream of wrestling's toughest grapplers, not even allowing herself to be bullied by WWF corporate owner Vince McMahon. It was McMahon who turned the traditional wrestling world upside down when he took over his father's business and brought together most of the nation's competing wrestling circuits into one gigantic and seemingly unstoppable megacorporation. McMahon likely sees something of himself in the woman who challenged the odds and did the impossible. He once had to struggle to beat the odds himself, facing down his own father as well as a billionaire cable tycoon, and so must see a kindred spirit in the warrior queen. Her success was not easily won or easily accepted. But she stands at the pinnacle long after her doubters have faded away.

If we as a society are to be honest with ourselves, we must admit that the odds are definitely against a woman making it in this rampaging man's world. One example is a 1997 poll in the magazine *Pro Wrestling Illustrated*, one of the many periodicals dedicated to following the crazy ups and downs in the sport, in which the readers were asked: "Can women's wrestling thrive again in the U.S.?"

These hard-core fans took a dim view of the future, 78 percent of them saying no. Four out of five fans could not conceive of a time when women's wrestling would be a reality, instead of mere window dressing. Such a lack of vision must be disheartening to Joanie Laurer, but she's never let it slow her down.

So the numbers tell us that Chyna is a female champion in a world that obviously isn't ready for that idea. But Joanie Laurer obviously doesn't care, and she proclaims that loudly every time she climbs over the top rope to grapple in the ring. Her immense skills make a lie of the claim that in wrestling, women cannot compete with men. In a world of jiggling valets and half-naked "ladies," she has taught us all that there is much more to being a woman in wrestling than having large breasts, a high-paid hairstylist, and a barely-there costume. In a field full of silicone pretenders, our Chyna is a fighter, not a poser. On *E! Extra*, Joanie said that she considers herself "an act of talent instead of eye candy." For those wrestling fans with discriminating taste, however, she is actually both.

Chyna stands alone at the summit, demanding our respect, insisting on our admiration, and demolishing any unfortunate men who happen to get between her and her goals. She is an inspiration to both the current crop of wrestling femmes and any young girls who might be considering coming after her to form the next generation of women wrestlers.

Chyna was never one to be shy about describing her unique place in the world of wrestling. She once used a sports entertainment metaphor on MTV's *Timeout* in order to paint us a vivid mental picture. She announced with pride and daring: "Chyna is to the WWF what the ball is to basketball."

Like Babe Didrikson to golf, like Billie Jean King to tennis, like Helen Gurley Brown to *Cosmopolitan*, so is Chyna to the field of professional wrestling.

She is an inspiration not only to those of us who watch from the cheap seats, but also to those peers (though can they really be called that?) with whom she shares the arenas as well. Tori, currently allied with the wrestler they call Kane, the Big Red Machine, in the WWF, has explained what she has learned from years of watching Laurer in action. With every match, Tori says, a loud and clear message is sent that "women can be physical and we can do the moves men do. Chyna really set precedents and showed that it could be done."

The Fabulous Moolah, always an outspoken, acerbic, and often controversial commentator on the state of the field she loves, expressed it this way. Looking around despairingly at the current crop of female representation in the field, she has said: "I think there's a need for woman wrestlers—but women *wrestlers*."

One thing is for sure. For as long as Chyna is on the card, the Fabulous Moolah—and the millions and millions of the rest of the world's wrestling fans—need never be disappointed.

# CHAPTER 2

# I DREAM OF JOANIE

All good fairy tales begin with "Once upon a time," and since any story that ends with a little girl growing up to be the Queen—albeit Queen of the Ring—must be classified as a fairy tale, then that is how this story should begin. So . . .

Once upon a time, in the far away and long ago of 1970, a slightly belated Christmas present arrived in the Laurer household. On December 27 of that year little Joanie Laurer was born in Rochester, New York. This little bit of birthday trivia should help you should you ever come face-to-face with the woman who grew up to call herself Chyna, because she has made it quite clear that it's information she would not provide willingly herself. "Never ask a woman her age," she has said, "especially a jacked-up babe."

It is extremely doubtful that anyone could have predicted the heights to which that little baby girl would rise, considering that three decades ago, not only was the sport of wrestling not held in as high a regard as it is today, but at the same time no woman had yet come along who could force wrestling to take her on her own terms, rather than the other way around. Yes, it should never be doubted that there were female wrestling stars who were giants in those days, but at the same time they were known mostly to the inner circle of wrestling cognoscenti, rather than to the wider world at large.

The family life for this military brat was not a happy one, as her parents divorced when she was very young, creating an unsettled situation. She has described her childhood life, both at home and at school, as "very dysfunctional." But still, "I am the girl next door," was something Joanie once said while chatting with Jay Leno. As fame came to Joanie, the tabloids had an unfortunate field day with her past.

The woman behind Chyna tries not to volunteer much about her relationship with parents Joe and Tina. Having at last reinvented herself as a hero, she attempts to keep that more helpless part of the past as far behind her as possible. Her contact with her family has long been strained, though she has indicated that the thing she'd most hate to lose in life would be the close relationship she has maintained with her sister Kathy, who is five years her senior. Joanie considers older sister Kathy to be her best friend in the entire world, even though according to Joanie their personalities are completely different, as the future brawler was essentially raised by her sibling. Looking at this powerful specimen today, it's hard to think of the warrior queen Chyna as ever having been the baby of the family, but that is what she was, with both Kathy and older brother Ray (who is four years older, and now goes by the nickname Sonny) towering over her as a child.

Though she does not willingly bring up the matter herself, she will occasionally speak on the topic when asked. While taking part in a recent online chat when visiting in the UK, Joanie chose to answer a fan's pointedly raised question directly:

"I've no contact with my mother and father," she typed while communing in cyberspace, "my sis loves my fame, and my big bro is a really big wrestling fan and he thinks it's sooo cool."

Joanie's big sister Kathy was blessed with a similar body type to the Amazon champion, and as they grew to adulthood, the two would often work out together and compete as to how far they pushed themselves during their exercise regime.

Once Joanie became fascinated by the wrestling she saw on television, the two sisters began to wrestle throughout their house, playacting their role models. Together, they would fantasize about what a good tag team they would make someday. Though Joanie always encouraged her sister's possible career move, as of the writing of this book, for the elder of the Laurer girls, it was just a lark—there's no indication that Kathy Laurer has any serious intentions of following her famous sister into the ring. As great a gimmick as that would be to sell to the public (one can sense Vince McMahon drooling now), for the foreseeable future, Chyna stands alone.

It is odd to think of this fierce giant of a woman as once having been a typical little girl enjoying the gentle fruits of childhood, but she did. Her favorite stories when she was young were of *Winnie the Pooh*, and she owned many of the books from that classic series. To bring things down to hard reality, however, sister Kathy states that sadly, their home life was so chaotic that once, their mother threw out all of Joanie's Pooh possessions when the child was only ten.

That was just one more step in the toughening process designed to create a champion.

How did this woman who once professed a certain distaste for wrestling when she was younger become one of its dominating forces?

Her body made her do it.

As Joanie Laurer grew to womanhood, she was made fun of by many because of her broad shoulders and superior size. High school is not an easy time for any of us turning from boys and girls to men and women, but it was especially difficult for her. She was treated cruelly by her classmates. They were unwilling to easily accept her imposing presence. "Other guys were intimidated by me because I was so big" she has said, looking back, trying to make sense of the pain. "It was like their machismo was threatened."

Perhaps another sixteen-year-old might have used that family turmoil and societal rejection as a start for behavior that could lead quickly on a downward spiral. As we all know, the pressure-cooker environment of adolescence has damaged many. Some kids, unfortunately, become lost, and turn to drugs or alcohol, or lose themselves in criminal behavior. But the young woman behind the myth that is Chyna was one of the lucky ones, for she managed to put the strain of torment to one side and develop the toughness to withstand the pain. Even throughout that period of punishment, she received good grades in high school and always made the dean's list.

Then, in the midst of it all, still feeling like a

stranger in a strange land, there came the seminal moment of her life.

Joanie Laurer discovered bodybuilding.

Like Newton and his apple, all it took was one taste to divert her energies in the right direction. She soon discovered that she was a natural. Her genetic makeup took to the workout regimen as if her soft body had been lying dormant, waiting for this urging all along.

For many of us, there comes a time when we desperately wish to reinvent ourselves in either mind or body, and Laurer did so in the most literal of senses, building herself an amazing new form, muscle by muscle, with the sweat and tears of hours of hard work in the gym. Considering this metamorphosis, it seems fitting that Laurer has stated the one person she would liked to have a chance to have met before he died was Frank Sinatra, for just like the crooning Chairman of the Board, she has exuded the attitude "I've Got to Be Me" all through her life.

But unfortunately, there was to be still more anguish before the good times finally came. Once she started lifting weights seriously, nasty new taunts were added to the old. Now, in addition to being made fun of for her size, naysayers began questioning her very sexuality, using that as an additional punishing weapon. She started being called a lesbian due to her interest in building herself a better body. Because at that time (in some ways only yesterday, but in others a million years away) women rarely worked out and it was not yet accepted as fit and proper, even her parents had difficulty in understanding their daughter and her critical choice. But Joanie kept at it regardless, even as the word "dyke" rang in her ears. Even today, she can still hear the words fly, usually from the mouths of wrestling fans uncomfortable with a woman competing on an equal playing field. But thanks to her success, she wears a tougher suit of emotional armor now, and the sting is lessened.

We all have multiple paths laid out before us that could lead to different lives, and the future Chyna was no exception to this life rule. Joanie had other varied interests in high school that might have led to other entertainment careers. She participated enthusiastically in the high school orchestra, where she played the cello. She is also said to be quite good on the flute. She sang, took part in numerous statewide musical competitions, and as a young woman was part of a band with people she considered "old geezers." When performing with that group, she would wear her hair long, a look that would seem unusual to her many fans today, and sing songs not only sung by her favorite, Frank Sinatra, but also by the likes of Billie Holiday and Tony Bennett. (Those traditional song stylists have always been the sort of music makers who appealed to Laurer. Asked her opinions of Elvis, this woman, who externally has at least shared his love of black leather, once said, "I didn't like Elvis. Elvis should leave the building.") Garbed in her colorful, sparkling dresses, such a contrast to her current basic black, she would steal the show. She could have pursued the musical world professionally if she so chose, so that today she'd be winning Grammys instead of Championship belts, but that was not to be. Laurer quickly decided that her personal and professional goals were not being met on that particular stage, and so she moved on to the pursuit we all know her for today. Witnesses who have been lucky enough to hear her warble backstage report that her voice is still good, so who knows? Maybe we'll all have a chance to hear it for ourselves someday.

Body building was not her only love and joy during the early years. During her high school days, Laurer also excelled at gymnastics as well as track and field, her finely honed body serving her well in both these pursuits. It is intriguing and a good indicator of her personality that both of these sports focused in on individual achievement, rather than on any sort of cooperative team effort. Laurer, with her unyielding goals, dreams, and ambitions, has never fit comfortably as part of a group. She faced little true physical competition over the years, and so she found that the best thing she could measure herself against was herself. There was no more exacting competitor than that. Though over the years as Chyna she has occasionally teamed with many others for brief periods of time—whether it be Triple H, D-Generation-X, or the Corporation—it has always been obvious to her audience that she has been her own woman, working her own agenda even while presenting the facade of doing it for others. Those partnerships she has temporarily forged have always benefited herself first and the team second.

As she pursued these varying fitness regimes, she always ate right, knowing the proper fuel to power her ambitious pursuit. To keep herself fit, no fast food burgers passed between the lips of this future champion. She still manages to stay away from those quick fixes to her hunger, an even more difficult task today in a life led mainly on the road. "You'd be surprised by what I eat," Laurer has said, indicating that to keep up her massive frame, eating was almost an all day event. To maintain her weight, her menu now includes protein shakes, vitamin supplements, and lots of orange juice.

Her love of foreign languages took her abroad in high school, giving her a chance in yet another new environment to discover just who Joanie Laurer was. As usual, one of her many interests earned her the ticket out. Fluent in Spanish, she went to Spain to take part in a six-month-long study program funded by a United Nations scholarship. It was a chance for Joanie to measure herself against a brand-new world, and she loved it. But nothing lasts forever. Eventually time ran out and she was due to return to the States, but her love of that friendly country and its people was so great that she found she could not bear to instantly return. She knew that her life's journey required more time to season, so she needed to figure out a way to stay in that country and continue with her high school education while living and working overseas. She was able to get a job there as a waitress to pay her expenses, just one of many mundane working experiences that Joanie has experienced on the road to success. She traveled extensively during that extended overseas period, moving through Europe, with four nights in France, two months in Germany and varied stays of differing lengths in other countries. Months turned into years, and by the time her walkabout was over she had ended up completing her high school education overseas.

Her unusually striking looks always caused her difficulty. Her unique physical gifts did not match well with society's traditional views of women. As she told the world on *Inside Edition* and elsewhere, her size had always made her an outcast. She was a square peg struggling to fit in a round hole. She faced a prejudice that tried to tell her that her unique differences were bad, instead of special qualities to be celebrated. Since her physical condition was beyond compare, she would time and again enter beauty contests, only to be told by promoters and competitors that even that world had no place for her. Her body type was not considered traditional enough, which was a difficult thing to hear, but Laurer did not despair. With the unwavering confidence of a champion, she altered her goals and began to appear instead in fitness competitions, where her singular talents were recognized. She did well competitively, an early success that gave a boost to her determination to succeed.

In 1987, she chose to enroll in the University of Tampa, where she had won a scholarship earned thanks to her extensive language skills. There, she matriculated toward a degree in

Spanish literature—which might explain why she was able to converse so easily with the Spanish wrestling correspondents who sat ringside one night on a Monday night *RAW is War,* startling them with her unexpected knowledge. Most wrestlers attempt to hide their college degrees, and usually do so well, since it doesn't sync with their public faces, so it might come as a surprise to many to learn that Joanie Laurer graduated from college with a double major in Spanish literature and can speak several languages, including Spanish, French, German, and Czech. She was still continuing to build herself for the future she knew was waiting, and in 1996, prior to her entering the wrestling arena where she would find her greatest success, her photos began to appear in *Women's Physique World* and other such magazines.

While in college, the lure of government service called, and she interned for the U.S. Secret Service, at a time when being a government intern had not yet become fodder for the queasy jokes of late-night talk show hosts. Other national organizations that got a taste of Chyna were American States and U.S. Aid. At the time, she had not yet heard the call to wrestling. She was toying with the idea of becoming an athletic trainer for the secret service, or maybe even a bilingual agent herself. Joanie could have been our first female James Bond! As with so many other things, she excelled in her education. When she finally graduated from the University of Tampa, doing so in a remarkable two years instead of four, she had a grade point average of 3.8.

After graduating from college in 1992, her next stop was to join the Peace Corps. Her assignment took her south to Costa Rica. She hoped that this broadening experience would make her seem more appealing as she pursued her then fervent goal of eventually getting a foreign diplomatic job. As she tried to decide what to do after that with her superb body and mind, it is reported that she dabbled in a wide variety of jobs, from bartender to belly dancer to delivering singing telegrams to selling beepers. For a time, she was even an airline attendant. One sight we can only imagine but desperately wish we could have seen is Joanie dealing with a rowdy passenger. If her rough treatment of her opponents in the ring is any indication, anyone who got out of line in the air might have found himself locked in an overhead luggage compartment!

While all this was going on, she continued religiously with her weightlifting regimen, working out heavily, as she had done during her college years. She is now so much at home in the gym that from this perspective it seems her entire life. "I'd been playing sports and lifting weights for as long as I can remember," she has said, and that dedication would shortly pay off for her. The rewards were not far off.

The first link in the chain that would lead her to the professional success she enjoys today was fitness promoter Kenny Kassell. Kassell changed her life. Laurer met him while involved in the exhausting fitness competition circuit, and it was to him that she first opened up to express an interest in professional wrestling. When he learned that she was considering moving off from the fitness life in that direction, he encouraged her, and tried to find someone who would take her under his wing in that strange new business.

Kassell led Joanie to Randy Powell, who had founded the PGWA (Professional Girl Wrestling Association) not that much earlier. Together, the three of them looked for a trainer worthy of the promising newcomer. Even that was not as easy as it seemed, not even for as superb a raw talent as Laurer. Since she knew next to nothing about pro wrestling other than what she saw on television from the vantage point of a fan, she was as green as they come. The fitness background and experience that Laurer brought to the table was not impressive to the seasoned wrestling vets. They did not want to take the time to try to mold Laurer. But the trio refused to give up, and kept seeking a mentor willing to invest in Joanie.

"All hope was not lost," Powell has said of that time. "I still had faith that she would get some training somewhere."

That training would come at the infamous hands of one of wrestling's greatest legends, who would give generously of his time and energy so that a new wrestling legend could be born.

That training would come at the hands of the man they called "Killer."

# CHAPTER 3

# WRESTLING WITH THE FUTURE

In the world of rock and roll, when you hear the nickname "Killer," you think of only one man: Jerry Lee Lewis, famous for the hit song "Great Balls of Fire." In the world of wrestling, however, when you hear the tag "Killer," that can only mean Walter Kowalski, whose own fame comes from stunts such as once ripping off an opponent's ear during a match.

The legendary Walter "Killer" Kowalski wrestled aggressively for over twenty-six years before retiring in 1977. Though record keeping was not an exact science during those early days of the sport, it is estimated by those who know best that this son of Polish immigrants competed in over six thousand matches. The famous story of the grisly time in 1954, that a knee drop to Yukon Eric savagely severed his ear helped give "Killer" an unmatched reputation for sadism. When

Kowalski, attempting to make amends, paid a visit to the downed Eric afterward in the hospital to wish him well, he found the sight of Eric's bandaged head so ridiculous that he could not stop laughing, making things worse. The event was witnessed by the wrestling reporters of the time, and greatly contributed to Kowalski's renown as a hardcore grappler. Kowalski fought all the major stars of his day, from Gorgeous George to Nature Boy Buddy Rogers, and is considered to be one of the greatest wrestlers of all time.

After the decades of pounding in the ring became too much for him, as it eventually does for all wrestlers, Kowalski retired from active battle to open the Killer Kowalski Institute for Professional Wrestling in Massachusetts. At the time that Joanie was casting about looking for a mentor, Big John Studd was perhaps the most famous of his students, though that was a fame that Chyna has surely by now surpassed with her own.

So it was perhaps inevitable that Joanie Laurer would connect with the former Hall of Famer at his school in Malden, Massachusetts, where together they would forge the popular persona under which she first wrestled. In the cold of New England, Joanie Laurer was set aside, and a new

Joanie was born, ready for the ring—Joanie Lee.

But there was to be a bump in the road before Joanie was on her way. About to enroll in his physically punishing class, Joanie had second thoughts. She asked the wrestling legend if she could first try out a few moves in the ring before making a decision on whether to plunk down her money. Learning from Kowalski would not be cheap, and she didn't want to risk her limited dollars on the course if she judged herelf and thought she would not be physically up to the challenge.

Kowalski's response was short and forceful, as usual for the champion. "You either do it or you don't!" So for a short while, she didn't.

Joanie went back home, trying to decide what she wanted to do next with her life. But she didn't want to have to look back on the past always wondering whether she was good enough. Her talents needed to be tried. Her curiosity got the better of her, and she decided that whatever it took, she would test herself at the school, under the tutelage of Kowalski. She returned to Massachusetts and signed up, along with three men who took perverse delight in continually telling her that a woman had no right to be there. "There were people who told me I was ugly, that I looked like a man," she said. "I thought that it would be different in wrestling. It would be a place where I found my niche."

Because of the initial reluctance of the male students around her, it did not seem as if that would be true, but she was amazed to discover at week's end, that even though she'd had to endure their scorn, it had strengthened her. She had survived while they packed up and went home. Joanie has always demonstrated a hardy determination to ignore the verbal slights and blows of those around her, and that well-earned toughness today serves her well in the role of Chyna.

"She was always hardworking and very pleasant to be around," Kowalski has said of those early times. "I am happy to have been a part of her formative years in the business."

Bizarrely, Kowalski, who changed the face of wrestling with Chyna, the Ninth Wonder of the World, and other well-known students, almost changed the face of late night television as well.

All was revealed to the public when the warrior queen appeared on *The Tonight Show with Jay Leno* on February 11, 2000. She was dressed in a tight-fitting black outfit, with a miniskirt and showing plenty of cleavage, creating an effect that would have made the Cat Woman look like a frump in comparison. In his conversation with Joanie, the jut-jawed host and former comedian admitted to the strange near-miss detour that his comedy career almost took thanks to the "Killer."

"When I wanted to go into comedy, I went to see his manager," Leno admitted of his early days, giving an imitation of a Kowalski grunt. "I walked into his office and he had a cardboard cutout of Killer. And he wanted me to be the comedy wrestler. He would say, 'you'll get a guy in a headlock, you whisper a joke in his ear, the guy would fall down laughing, and you'll pin him.' " Everybody's got to have a gimmick, or so goes the song, but from the sound of it, it's a good thing that Leno passed that one by . . . though David Letterman might have wished otherwise.

One witness to history with many fond memories of the early Joanie is photographer Michael Lano. Lano has been shooting pro wrestling events since the early days of 1966,when he got involved as a favor to a friend who was running the Los Angeles territory, back in the pre-Vince days when the U.S. was still divided up into wrestling circuits. As a teenager, he started flying around to all of the competing territories, and then branched out to the fabled international federations, shooting in Japan and Mexico since 1968. Fans will certainly be aware of his popular long-running syndicated wrestling TV (*Canvas Cavity*) and radio

(*Squared Circle*) shows, which have given an insider's glimpse behind the glitz and glamour that is pro wrestling. But Lano has another life as well. He isn't ashamed to admit that it was from the sale of pro wrestling photography that he financed his education through dental school. And because of his love of the sport, he has given back his talents to those who gave so much to him. Since most of the wrestlers taking chair shots to the face have no dental insurance, they frequently call on Lano to repair what the rigors of wrestling have undone. This reconstructive work has earned him the nickname Dr. Mike. Ring Celebrities from Madusa to "Rowdy" Roddy Piper to Mick Foley (aka the tremendously popular Cactus Jack and Mankind) and Sabu have been in his chair. As a result of all this time with camera in hand, Lano was one of the few back there at the beginning during Joanie's early days before she turned pro.

"She trained right about the same time as Paul Levesque and Perry Saturn and John Chronus," he explained to the author in an exclusive interview. "They were all in the same school class of Walter 'Killer' Kowalski. She was a very good kid. She had short red hair, and had the bodybuilder gimmick, which Walter Kowalski, who has always been a friend to the WWF, kept trying to push, saying, 'I have the next big thing. I've got the next big thing.' He's provided the WWF with so much of their talent.

"He did well training her. She was a little green. When I first met her at her first and second matches with Kowalski in front of people, she was a babyface, trying to get the crowd to clap and go for her. She was very friendly, but a little bit stiff, a little bit green."

Chyna fans today, familiar with her tough, hard image, would be surprised to see how much the champion has changed in just a few short years. That good girl image which she once capitalized on is long behind her. Joanie the beginner knew that before she could make it in the big leagues, she needed more experience. But she already came to the table with so much that her period of apprenticeship was not very long at all.

"She said, 'Can you get me booked into Japan, because I know I've got to go to the next step with my training,' " recalls the effusive Lano. "And basically she never had to work anywhere else. They never took her to Memphis, which WWF typically does. They never sent her to a farm school so she could get in front of people. She went pretty much straight after two and a half years with Kowalski right into being put as the valet for Hunter. She was very eager to learn, very eager to seek out advice. She would always bug me to see the Japanese pro wrestling magazines. And there aren't that many pro women who are that dedicated. So she had a real natural aptitude for the business, I would say.

"She never worked as Chyna anywhere else until she debuted with the WWF. That's a testament to her skills. Because she was a track star and a real true athlete, and for whatever other reasons, she didn't have to go to any farm school or do any developmental stuff. *Boom!* She was just there because she was impressive. She was the first woman with a huge bodybuilder physique to come into wrestling."

That bodybuilding background born of years of hard work served her in good stead when it came to performing ring action. "Very few men can lift as much as she, dead lift and power lift. They don't even bill it, but she is one of the strongest women on the planet. Actually, she outlifts Hunter. She's very impressive with the squats and all the things that she's done. She's the first to seek out a gym, that much I'll say—when she comes into town, even if she's a little too busy to talk, she'll say, 'Where's the gym?' even before the other wrestlers do. So she's very religious with the training."

As Chyna's unrivaled stature in the field has grown, it was difficult to stay in touch, but Lano indicated that there were still times when his own peculiar talents have made for some interesting moments behind the scenes at the WWF. "Backstage at a house show, I pulled out all those photos, and she was groaning when I showed it to the other members of DX. 'I knew that your photos would come out to haunt me.' I was literally the only one who took those pictures. Those pictures have appeared in all the tabloids in 1999 of how she used to look before all the extensions and dyeing the hair black and all of that. All of those DX guys grabbed every old picture of her that they could to tease her.

"She's certainly made people forget about Sable, who never even had any aptitude for it," Lano said, when asked of Joanie's place in the wrestling pantheon and the effect that she has had on the industry. (Sable is the stage name of Rena Mero, who left the WWF under a cloud, claiming sexual harassment. Mero has since been seen in the pages of *Playboy*, acting on the Sci Fi Channel show *First Wave* and elsewhere.) "Joanie grew up watching it, she grew up watching Bruno Samartino and Killer Kowalski and Captain Lou Albano. Those were her three favorites. She grew up watching the business, and she deserves all of what she's getting now that she's worked so hard for it. There's a lot of sacrifice on her part. It's not easy. I don't think the fans know how difficult it is. She was off-camera when she had her jaw broken and her chin reset because she had what we call a prognathic chin. She's a real good sport. She's done an awful lot. She's had orthodontics and teeth bleaching and gone through quite a bit of plastic surgery to please the WWF and the fans and make herself more marketable. It's a lot of dedication. Being off-camera for a couple of months was very hard for her. Because as she describes it, when she'd get that fever being in front of people, it's hard to give that up, and they do it twenty-four-seven, three-hundred-and-sixty-five days a year."

Joanie showed a remarkably calm demeanor when being asked about these medical issues in a recent online chat for the readers of *MegaStar* in the U.K. During the apparently unmoderated chat, while screens full of vulgar and insulting comments were being bandied about, as is common for events of this type, she managed to keep her cool—whereas in the ring, if Jeff Jarrett or Chris Jericho had spoken to her in such a way, she would have been tossing their bodies about immediately. She had this to say of the surgery that she has had done to improve her body in a way that natural means such as exercise could not: "Of course I've had my boobs done. But my jaw was a medical condition because of an over-bite. It turned out looking really well. I did it for me. I feel confident. I had a hard body, and I was stuck behind a hard face. I would do it five times over."

On *The Tonight Show with Jay Leno*, she could even joke about the matter, indicating that she even thought of her surgery as a form of investment, the way we normal mortals consider IRAs and 401Ks. "Everytime I do an interview lately," she said with a bright smile, "everybody says, 'Are your breasts real?' And then of course I go, 'What do *you* think?' But I look at it now as a real estate investment, because I figure all these women are selling their implants now." Joanie was referring to other female ring personalities who have profited from the sale of removed implants, surely one of the oddest souvenirs to ever come into being on the collectors' market. "Five years down the road, after I've done a whole bunch of great stuff, I figure I'll sell them on eBay." Though she makes such a claim in jest, all indications are that Joanie Laurer is too classy a lady to go down that road.

One of the things that Lano most appreciates

about Joanie is her own appreciation of the long history of ring prowess, her recognition that the sport did not begin with her, something rare in a field populated by people who feel they have no time to look back. He brings up the background of recent newcomers to the ring, another Kowalski protégé, as an example. "Prince Albert was supposed to have come in as a George the Animal Steele sort of character, because he's got such a hairy back. He was going to be called Son of Steele, which actually Hunter and Chyna liked. They embraced a lot of Kowalski's people. And Joanie in particular never forgot where she came from. They're always very nice and gracious to Killer Kowalski, who is a definite legend in the WWF."

And being the person most look to when they think of women in wrestling, Joanie has not lost sight of those legends who came before her. "She was very loyal to Fabulous Moolah and Mae Young, who run something called the LIWA [Ladies International Wrestling Association]. When Joanie started training, she said, 'I want to send in my dues and be part of women's wrestling.' She's more about women's wrestling than the catfight stuff. From what I know, she kind of abhors it. Because the catfights are with women who aren't really trained wrestlers and

40

don't take the time to learn how to take proper bumps and stuff, like a Sable or a Debra or Miss Kitty, people like that who are just basically valets. Joanie was never brought up to be a valet, but a lady wrestler. She abhors that and she supports the longtime tradition of women wrestlers who were very big in the fifties.

"She's helping by making her contributions and having done things for LIWA in the past to help fund a retirement home and a Hall of Fame for legitimate women wrestlers like Moolah and Mae Young and people like that. Joanie has an active interest (and always has had) in protecting the heritage of women's wrestling. She hangs around with Mae and Moolah quite a bit, whereas the other young women in wrestling don't really care so much about it. They weren't classically trained as athletically legitimate women pro wrestlers. She's still palling around with Mae and Moolah. She and Pat Patterson are sort of responsible for why Mae and Moolah are there. Joanie always tries to carry the tradition on, and to this day she's trying to learn everything she possibly still can from Mae and Moolah."

With her physique, her winning personality, and known affiliation with Kowalski, she was immediately noticed by the fans as she competed in various women's wrestling leagues. She wrestled with the PGWA (Professional Girl Wrestling Association) and LIWA. When she attended the LIWA annual convention in Las Vegas in June of 1996, she was immediately embraced by those who would so quickly become her peers. They knew that she had hooked up with the fabled trainer, and that was good enough for them. Joanie was amazed by the warm welcome that they gave her. As she began her ring career, her skills were recognized so quickly by the fans and her peers that she was named the PGWA Rookie of the Year.

As Joanie Lee, she looked nothing like the menacing Chyna. Instead of the basic Goth black that is her usual attire today, she was garbed in a cheerful red, white, and blue outfit. Rather than the raven tresses we now admire, she was an innocent-seeming redhead. She toured the many independents, wrestling in such venues as the Universal Wrestling Federation. She knew that other stars, such as Riptide, had been created there, and she hoped that the magic that had worked for them would work for her. She worked hard on that circuit, eventually battling Riptide herself in Daytona at the end of her tour. Riptide was also a bodybuilder, and the sight of the two of them in the ring was breathtaking. Joanie went into that confrontation with an undefeated record and was lucky enough to come out the same way. Making that win helped put Joanie Lee on the map.

In the fall of 1996, Joanie continued to wrestle for such circuits, but that was not enough of a payoff for her. Her ambition was as great as her strength, and she was one strong woman. She wanted to play in the big leagues. With some, such an unbridled desire might be seen as hubris after so short a training period, but with such a rare individual as Joanie, it only made sense to move on and up.

But the opportunities for such a big woman were limited. She was so devastating a figure, slashing a swath of destruction in her wake, that she soon ran out of women with whom to compete. By the dint of those years of hard work, she had transformed herself into such a strong opponent that they just wouldn't get in the ring with her! Laurer became so desperate to compete that she was sometimes forced to resort to subterfuge. At one point, having run out of women grapplers who would give her sufficient competition, she slicked her hair back, donned a binding bodysuit so that no one would know that she was a woman, and started competing against men. The sport had gotten so deeply into her blood to the point that she was willing to do almost anything to wrestle.

In her search of the next big opportunity, she would travel to whatever arena she could find that held an independent event, and leave her portfolio behind for the promoter. She wanted to get noticed, though looking at her physique now, it's a wonder that there ever could have been any trouble. Long before her talents were fortuitously recognized by the WWF and her contract picked up, she'd even recorded an interview and audition tape that she had forwarded to Eric Bischoff of the WCW, asking him for a shot at joining that federation. But Bischoff foolishly took a pass, and the world has never been the same. (Nor has Bischoff's career. Once the moving force and the top onscreen executive for the WCW, Bischoff took a nosedive in status as the result of the WCW's continued trouncing by the WWF in the ratings. Perhaps if he had paid more attention to that unsolicited tape years back, things would have gone differently for him.)

The odds seemed to be against her. No one wanted to take a chance on a woman who wrestled like a man, with a man's aggressiveness and a man's fervor. Also, it should be noted that up until Joanie Laurer came on the scene and was able to achieve her success as Chyna, no female bodybuilder before her had ever been able to make the successful transition from one sport to another. Women could wrestle, that had been happening since the beginning—but muscular women were considered a taboo in the wrestling field, as they were not considered sexy enough to draw in the predominantly male audience. The men in the audience wanted to be able to at least pretend to themselves, though they might never say it out loud, that they could dominate the wrestling woman, if given the chance. With Chyna, no such pretense was possible. The audience of the day unfortunately mirrored the wider world at large. That Chyna has not appeared on the cover of *Cosmopolitan* or *Vogue* is society's problem, not hers. They expected women to simply be eye candy, taking the more submissive role of valets or managers. That was how the pre-Chyna wrestling world looked at women.

Chyna was the woman who would change all that, perhaps the only woman with the capabilities of doing so, turning the preconceptions of the wrestling world upside down. At the time, she hoped to wrestle the then-WCW women's champion, Madusa Macelli, but to her frustration she was turned down. The muscular Amazon type was just not considered a marketable product in those days, and no matter how many doors she tried to open, they just

slammed shut on her. But she persisted.

With the pro wrestling options apparently so limited, she took out insurance on her future by also obtaining the training to be a professional boxer. She studied for a period of time under the guidance of Mike Peabody of Lawrence, Massachusetts. For some reason, things seemed to move more swiftly for her in that arena. She already had her first professional bout scheduled with another woman in February 1997 when she was called to the big-time by the WWF. Her love of that pastime is so great that she has said on many occasions that her favorite sport (as opposed to the "sport entertainment" that is wrestling) is boxing, and that her favorite athlete is Mike Tyson. Thanks to the success of her eventual career, she got a chance to meet Tyson face-to-face. Her response to meeting this fellow champion was to say that based on what she had known of his public persona, she was surprised by how sweet the heavyweight champion seemed. But so it is with any public figure, and Chyna's fans too have discovered the same about her when meeting her outside of the ring. She only plays the part of the she-devil when within the walls of the world's largest arenas. Otherwise, the sweetness of Joanie Laurer still shines through.

Joanie has built her body through sheer determined effort, but it is for herself that she has done this, and not for you. She doesn't mind if men ogle her and women want to be her, but that's not why she worked so long and hard to build her well-toned body. Whether beating you at arm-wrestling, or bench pressing more than most men—a reported 365 pounds with a mid-400 pound deadlift—she has created herself for herself.

But she had a dilemma with what she created. She had become such a dominating force in women's wrestling that she had run out of worthy opponents to face. For a while it looked as if the role of Chyna would be nipped in the bud before it had even begun.

So it's a good thing for both her and us that she ran into a wrestling villain who had dubbed himself Triple H.

# CHAPTER 4

# H MARKS
# THE SPOT

It would be difficult if not impossible to tell the story of Joanie Laurer aka Chyna, the Ninth Wonder of the World, without also telling the story of her counterpart, Paul Levesque aka Hunter Hearst Helmsley aka the reigning heel of all heels, Triple H.

In the ring, Chyna and Triple H seem bound together by a special gravity, whether their imaginative storylines have propelled them together or pushed them temporarily apart. Outside of the ring they have a special bond that few wrestlers—in fact, few people for that matter—have been able to achieve.

As Triple H. Levesque's often repeated tagline is "I am the Game," and with both his moves and words, he lives up to that pronouncement every week. There are few who would dare argue with him. After all, who would want to tangle with the man who recently won his second WWF Heavyweight title at the Unforgiven pay-per-view event in Charlotte, North Carolina, on September 26, 1999. In this business there are heroes, known in insider lingo as "faces," or "babyfaces," and there are villains, who are known as "heels." Though wrestlers have always been able to have long and successful careers as either faces or heels, sometimes turning from one to the other in midcareer to get a popularity boost, or in fact turning many times, traditionally the heroes were always cheered and the villains were roundly booed. In recent years, however, we have gotten away from that longstanding tradition. There has been an odd turnabout, as villains started being cheered as loudly as the heroes. We've come all the way from family-friendly role model Hulk Hogan telling kids to eat their vitamins to Stone Cold Steve Austin giving the boss the finger and chugging beers in the ring. It's a transformation that has worried the op-ed page pundits, largely people who have never been wrestling fans themselves, even as it has been hungrily embraced by the wrestling audience.

And in this strange new world of wrestling popularity to which we have evolved, where seven of the ten top-rated cable shows each week can be counted upon to be wrestling events,

Triple H has maneuvered himself like a master, showing an unmatched understanding of the way things work. With his greatest successes coming once Chyna bound herself to his side, he has become the heel we love to hate.

The six-feet-five-inch-tall, 279-pound Paul Levesque was born July 27, 1969 (just a year and a few months before Joanie Laurer), in Nashua, New Hampshire, though obviously the height and weight statistics differed greatly for him as a bouncing baby boy in the swinging sixties. As a child, he enjoyed wrestling on the playgrounds, a habit that did not particularly enamor him to teachers or fellow students. "When other kids were watching football, baseball, and basketball, I was watching professional wrestling," he admitted to Greg Oliver of *SLAM! Sports*. "My heroes growing up were different from everyone else's who weren't wrestling fans. Ric Flairs, and people like that." If only those who were made nervous by this early obsession had been able to see the future that awaited him, perhaps they would have turned to encouragement instead.

After pursuing a brief career as a bodybuilder, Levesque turned instead to the world of wrestling. The stories he'd been hearing of the high incomes that the most successful in that field earned were deeply seductive to him. The bodybuilding world seemed to have a salary ceiling that had become stifling. And he was determined that he was going to be one of those lucky few who would pummel his way to the top. Levesque was in luck, because his bodybuilding sponsor at the time, Ted Arcidi, had also performed in the past with the WWF. Together they worked at creating a buffer body that would capture the attention of the new world of wrestling, where muscled giants had replaced the old-fashioned amorphous maulers with monster guts.

After graduating from the Kowalski school as Joanie would later, Levesque was given the name Terra Ryzing by Kowalski himself. Reinvented as such, he wrestled for the IWF, based in New England. (The IWF was also owned by Kowalski.) The odd moniker Terra Ryzing was supposed to be, well, *terrorizing*, but to most the name just seemed silly, and it thankfully did not stick. But while wearing that name Levesque made his professional wrestling debut in 1992, and managed to win the IWF title the same year. As a tag team, he partnered with wrestler Perry Saturn, who has gone on to a successful career of his own, recently jumping to the WWF.

Levesque left the regional promotion after winning the title, and went over to Ted Turner's

World Championship Wrestling federation, which at the time was the destination of choice for an up-and-comer, as it was beating the WWF soundly in the ratings. If you were watching televised wrestling events in those days, you would have seen Ryzing's TV premiere in January 1994. He was forced to face off against Brian Armstrong, aka Jesse James, a popular wrestler with whom Levesque would have a long professional relationship later over at the WWF, continuing to this day. Ryzing won that first match, which was a surprise to many, as Jesse James had been given the push and was well-liked by the fans. But storylines do not always go the way even the most well-educated in these matters might think, and Ryzing quickly tied Armstrong in painful knots using the Indian Death Lock, forcing a quick submission.

But unfortunately for Levesque, the rest of his career did not follow the tenor of that first match, and though he fought well and often against many midranked opponents, the powers-that-be at Titan Sports seemed to be passing him over. He was hitting the same sort of wall that Joanie Laurer was facing, though in a different locale and under other circumstances. He wasn't getting the chances and attention that he felt his skills deserved, and when it came time for him to lose to Larry "Living Legend" Zbyzsko for the television title, he could see the handwriting on the wall. And he wasn't happy.

So he did what all wrestlers do when their characters seem to have grown stale with the public—they reinvent themselves! Since the beginning, when wrestlers have failed to go over with a fickle audience, they have changed their names, gimmicks, masks, nationalities, and makeup. And so Levesque knew, as he would have to have learned under Kowalski's tutelage, that there was always a chance for a second chance.

And so was born the carefully-planned persona of Jean-Paul Levesque, a raging fop supposedly of French-Canadian extraction. Snob was his middle name. Disdain dripped from every well-oiled pore of his body, and he did his best to make Joe Six-pack's blood boil. He wanted the crowd to hate him, and hate him with a passion.

He succeeded.

He would come out in foxhunting attire, playing off the "hate the rich" prejudice of the audience, and put off the crowd with his finely-honed aristocratic arrogance. It worked, yet it seemed (though he kept it to himself at the time) that he was not entirely comfortable with it. Years later, when asked to name one of the dumbest things that he'd ever heard, his swift response was that being told to be a Frenchman back in those early WCW days won the prize.

He played a character who was supposedly fabulously wealthy and too important to be dirtying his hands with the constant string of jobbers he was forced to battle. This haughty presentation consistently placed him on the bottom rung of popularity polls at the time. The fans hated him, but unlike today, they were not yet ready to love hating him. When he lost to Alex Wright at the 1994 Starrcade, it was rumored that he would soon tag team with Lord Steve Regal in a partnership that might help his popularity, but that was not to work out for him. True success for Paul Levesque did not arrive until he left behind him yet a second character in the dust.

Two chances were not enough. He was to have a third chance, and luckily for Levesque, the third time was the charm.

True success did not come to him until he jumped to the WWF, where over the past five years his character of Hunter Hearst Helmsley (more commonly known as Triple H, or simply HHH) has become increasingly more important with each passing month. He soon began taking a major role in the WWF storylines. He had at last figured out the proper personality that would captivate audiences as the ultimate villain. This time, the persona clicked. Though he still put off vibes of being better than you and me, the blueblood aspect receded a bit into the background. His reasons for feeling superior no longer seemed much attached to class or wealth as much as sheer conceit.

His insulting sneer seems etched in stone; it is rare to see him without a curved lip. It's a wonder that his face does not freeze that way. Chyna has said that one of the first things that she notices about people is their teeth, and with Hunter Hearst Helmsley, she would not be disappointed. Those teeth are all a part of a picture of a hunk of the bad boy variety. His finishing move, the Pedigree, is one of the most devastating and recognizable closers in wrestling, and has become one that has even been used by Chyna herself. The fans reacted favorably to the new Levesque.

His transformation from highbrow to lowlife worked.

Before allying himself with Chyna to achieve ultimate success, Triple H's plotlines were often entwined with Sable, the blond sexpot who played his valet. Sable, aka Rena Mero, is now more well known for her break from wrestling and for her lawsuit against the WWF than for the wrestling she did in the ring, but at the time, she seemed a good partner for the bad boy. It was only later, after the partnership had failed and Chyna had taken her place, that she defected and the complaints began. (On Joanie's appearance on *Live with Regis and Kathy Lee*, during which Chyna grappled with up-for-anything Regis in a makeshift ring, she gave her opinion on the stated reasons for Sable's swift departure from the world of wrestling—that Mero claimed that she was asked as Sable to enact storylines that she felt were personally degrading, which offended her as a woman and mother. Chyna indicated that from her own vantage point, the truth of the matter was otherwise—one could always exercise a veto whatever plots were suggested. Joanie did not want anyone to get the wrong idea about the actions she took both within the ring and outside of it. She wanted you to hear it, and hear it loud and clear—she was the one in control of her destiny, and always would be.)

Levesque's blueblood was set up against a good old country boy in an attempt to start a class war in the WWF that climaxed at the In Your House pay-per-view on December 17, 1995. In one of the more disgusting nonring locales that promoters had come up with, the two men were forced to compete in a filthy hog pen. Wrestling fans always want to see down-to-earth country beat smug city, and they were not disappointed.

Henry O. Godwinn won. But Levesque's important wins would come soon.

Levesque won his first Intercontinental Heavyweight crown by defeating then champion Marc Mero (husband of Sable) on October 21, 1996, in Terra Haute, Indiana. Wrestling successfully, he was able to hold onto that coveted title until the Rock took it away from him on February 13, 1997, in a blistering match in Providence, Rhode Island.

Like Joanie, he has been unwilling to sacrifice friendship on the altar of the party line. That led to an unfortunately detour on his road to the top.

His reinvention in the WWF had been successful, and he was scoring well with the fans, but his swift rise stalled out at New York's famed Madison Square Garden. It was already scheduled to be an eventful night, one containing not only a match in which Triple H was supposed to defeat Razor Ramon, but another in which Shawn Michaels was due to trounce Diesel before the two losers went off to the WCW (where they too would get the chance to reinvent themselves as Scott Hall and "Big Sexy" Kevin Nash, now known as the Outsiders). That's usually what happens when wrestlers jump ship—to get out of their contracts, they are often asked to go out as losers. That's what Jeff Jarrett did when he took his leave of the WWF, and what the Dudley Boyz had to do to get their way into the WWF from the ECW. (The initials ECW stand for the new kid on the block, Extreme Championship Wrestling, now seen on TNN and rapidly gaining in popularity as compared to the two majors. Which means, of course, that the majors are paying close attention and taking an interest in plucking some of their finest wrestlers.) The audience got the drama it expected that night, and more.

The expected champions Triple H and Shawn Michaels won exactly as planned, but once the matches were over, the unexpected happened. Instead of staying in character and spewing the standard wrestling vitriol at their vanquished opponents, Helmsley and Michaels confounded the audience by creating a moment of true disbelief—rather than a heckling, they gave their departing friends an ovation. A wall had been broken down between who they were supposed to be and who they actually were. The longtime coworkers had decided to say a very public goodbye. The four fast friends soon were laughing and hugging in the midst of the ring, the sort of sight that was supposed to be left backstage.

McMahon was reportedly livid that "kayfabe" (the insider term for the act of keeping up the illusion of reality that is wrestling) had been so blatantly broken, that the curtain had been dropped from between what was real and what was only playacting. Someone had to be made to pay for this breach of conduct. Unfortunately, as Michaels, also known as HBK, or the Heartbreak Kid, was the reigning champion, he was untouchable, and as both Hall and Nash were gone to greener pastures, it was Helmsley who was forced to face the wrath of the boss alone. And though Levesque had been able to defeat many mighty warriors in the ring, no one messes with the CEO. Apparently as punishment for his sins, he was stuck fighting the lesser lights of the federation until he was rescued from limbo with the help of his old friend Michaels. Along with Michaels himself, the newly invented Chyna was to be a part of that solution—the creation of a group of wrestlers who would be called D-Generation-X, whose goal was to destroy the reigning order of the WWF. That played well with the fans, who wanted to see McMahon get put in what they thought was his proper place..

Without Chyna's role in that group, Helmsley might not have gotten to the summit he now occupies. In addition to being a two-time WWF Intercontinental Champion, he is also a two-time WWF European Champion, the 1997 King of the

Ring, and additionally the current champion as of this writing, having won the WWF heavyweight title from Mankind on August 23, 1999. (To give some idea of the fast-paced world of wrestling, this is a belt that Mankind had held for just one day, having won it only the day before from Stone Cold Steve Austin.) Triple H is now so well-known and so capable of selling tickets that he was chosen as the headliner at the December 12, 1999, pay-per-view Armageddon.

As with anyone who has made it to the top of a profession, luck and timing have played a part in Levesque's success. This is not meant to slight his accomplishments, as chance does favor the prepared mind. With the Undertaker and Steve Austin both sidelined in recent months by injuries, Levesque has had the freedom and opportunity to be the consummate heel that the WWF needs to remain strong in the marketplace. The loss of the other two men has meant there was a void to be filled, and out of the endless army of muscle men, Triple H is the only character capable of rising to that challenge. His convoluted storylines in recent months have been the preeminent plots of the WWF, even leading him to "marry" Stephanie McMahon, daughter of the owner of the company (while real life partner Laurer watches on, knowng that wrestling often asks the strangest things of its participants). He has replaced Steve Austin as the WWF's main troublemaker, and will likely remain in that role of hellraiser until Austin has completed his recuperation. Even then, the Texas Rattlesnake might find himself in a bit of trouble upon his return, as Triple H's recent antics have solidly captured the public's imagination.

His ever-increasing fame has even helped him break out of the wrestling mold, propelling him into TV acting just as it did for Steve Austin before him (who went on to a regular gig there and seems on the verge of his own spin-off series). Levesque guest-starred on *The Drew Carey Show*, playing, of all things, a wrestler. In the episode entitled "Rats, Kate's Dating a Wrestler," which aired January 27, 1999, the regulars decided to hire a wrestler to endorse their brand of beer, and so Levesque was called in to portray the Disciplinarian, a grappler whose liking for the lager was a little too strong, resulting in ruining both his fictional wrestling career and the prospects for the beer. Though it was not much of a stretch, as he was playing what he was every day—though under a different name—Levesque must be commended for pulling off his first acting role with appeal, even with that typecasting, putting him into the exceedingly small group of wrestlers who can act without embarrassing themselves.

In addition to his recently demonstrated acting talents, Levesque has also shown himself to have a remarkable ability to see the future. When he was once asked, if given the chance, what he'd tell Monica Lewinsky, who was on everyone's mind at the time, he said he only had two words for her. These were not the standard D-Generation-X battlecry, but rather: "Jenny Craig." This was long before the former presidential intern took that bizarre route, becoming a Jenny Craig company spokeswoman, something most rational people would never have even dared to imagine.

One wonders whether his sharp powers of prognostication were working back when he made that important decision to hook up with Joanie Laurer, bringing her with him into the WWF, and garnering them both more success than they could ever have dreamed of back as green beginners in Killer Kowalski's camp.

# CHAPTER 5

# DYNAMIC DUO

Perhaps the collision of Triple H and Chyna was inevitable, but Joanie Laurer, who'd only known of Triple H from his obnoxious stage personality and the stories she had heard about him when he attended Kowalski's school before she did, had mixed feelings about this man who was considered to be the school's most successful student. Listening to her, one would easily assume that such a team-up was not meant to be.

"Between what I heard and the way I saw him act on TV, I thought he was the Antichrist," Laurer has said of those first perceptions of her future partner.

While Laurer was wrestling for other federations outside of the WWF, and hoping that opportunity would knock, the two met at a hotel bar to chew over the business. As is inevitable with anyone who ever knew the legendary wrestler and trainer who showed them the ropes, Laurer and Levesque began to swap their favorite Killer Kowalski stories. Levesque had graduated earlier, before Laurer signed up, and they each had plenty to say about the man. They talked about Laurer's problems, and in that bull session began to discuss a way that Laurer could break through the barriers that were keeping her down. Later, together with Triple H's tag-team partner and close friend, Shawn Michaels, the Heartbreak Kid, they came up with the basis of Joanie's new character. She would be a female manager and sidekick, tough as nails, but remaining sexy at the same time. She'd be strong enough to take on any man. She'd be more than just a wrestler, she'd be an event in her own right.

She'd be the Ninth Wonder of the World.

The story of Triple H was that he had been let down by every male wrestling superstar he'd tried to depend on, and so it was time to try something unusual. It would go over well with the fans, they were all sure of it.

Little did they know that this hastily conceived plan was to be more than just an attention-getting gimmick, that they would end up as soulmates.

But first they had to pitch it to the boss.

Vince McMahon didn't think it would work.

He was sure that the men whose livelihoods depended on appearing tough and unbeatable would never be willing to lose to a girl. He was afraid that his wrestlers, even though they were also his employees, would rebel, and be uncontrollable when faced with fighting a woman. For a while it looked as if Chyna would never be born.

Then fate stepped in. An injury put Shawn Michaels out of action for a while due to knee surgery, and Triple H was left with no partner. McMahon was stuck, and he was forced to let Chyna try against his better judgment, just so Levesque would have a partner, even though he was still worried that it would not go over well, either behind the scenes or in the ring. All told, it had taken them a year and a half from the time they first came up with the idea over drinks in a bar for the boss to allow them to put what they had dreamed up into practice.

First had to come the name. The tag Joanie Lee was to be put in mothballs. Now the name Chyna seems perfect to describe her, as we think of the homonym China as something large and powerful, but the warrior woman didn't always like the world-famous appellation that she now carries. "Chyna, the name, was picked for me," she has said, sounding resigned to it. "China says 'small, delicate.' I didn't like it much, but I've grown to love it."

While appearing years later on MTV's *True Life*, Joanie said of the search for the right persona that "all of our characters are a little bit of ourselves." Unlike some wrestlers, whom we hope evidence a wide disparity between their wide in-ring activities and their personal lives, with Chyna we appreciate the strong center that we see existing on stage, and hope that the woman behind it is just as strong.

Chyna first appeared to the public not as an employee of the WWF, but in the role of a fan, just like one of us. The true saga of Chyna all began while Triple H was battling Goldust for the Intercontinental title on Monday night's *RAW is War* in February 1997. The action was proceeding furiously when, all of a sudden, viewers were shocked to see a brawny female behemoth who had been sitting at ringside, name as yet unknown to them, reach out and manhandle Marlena, Goldust's manager. (In the spirit of reinvention, Marlena has also gone through some changes, and is known to today's wrestling fans as the shapely Teri Runnels.) This large female interloper was ostensibly a mere viewer just like themselves, one perhaps made overexcited by the furious action of event. Security had to pry the woman we now know as Chyna away from the cigar-smoking manager. With great difficulty they ejected her from the arena. It was a decidedly different debut, and fans did not know where it would lead. Would they see this woman again?

They did, and they were glad. She purportedly bailed herself out of jail after this incident and showed up at the next spot on the WWF circuit. Once more she showed a particular interest in the matches of Triple H, and again leapt out to attack the petite Marlena. Most fans would know better than to get involved in the action ("Kids, don't try this at home!"), but this one showed no such common sense. Leaping the barricades designed to separate *us* the fans from *them* the professionals, Chyna delivered another devastating whipping. This playacted feud went on for weeks, and when it was finally over, it was the team of Goldust and Marlena who were hurt, and not the talented newcomer. Triple H took notice of this, and then was able to put into effect what had been his and Joanie's underlying plan all along—getting Chyna into the business as his bodyguard. From that moment the two were inseparable. When Triple H was due to battle Goldust at the March 23, 1997, Wrestlemania, he chose Chyna to debut as his bodyguard, and a new dynamic duo was born.

When asked to explain why he'd chosen to ally himself with such a woman, Levesque immediately praised her fighting skills. "She proved to me that she'd take a whack at any man or woman, regardless of the circumstances," he said.

The team handled the public aspects of their roles exceedingly well also. In fact, when one interviewer suggested that there was perhaps no accident in their coming together, but rather that it had instead been scripted based on the two of them actually knowing each other through Kowalski's school prior to her debut, Helmsley made a great show of vigorously denying it. When the questions continued to persist, and a reporter let drop that it was Killer Kowalski himself who was the one who had spilled the information, Helmsley exploded. He questioned Kowalski's sanity and violently ended the interview. Both Levesque and Laurer knew that the role was always paramount, even when bits of reality based on their burgeoning real-life relationship were allowed to slip in.

Even with all the hard work that had gone on before, Chyna's true training only started when she began to work in the WWF in February 1997. Just like the early Beatles at The Cavern, she went to Germany for her first real break. She spent sixteen days touring with the other wrestlers. It was apparently just like living in a college dorm surrounded by a bunch of men who according to Joanie were typically "farting and burping." In fact, Laurer has said that the other wrestlers wouldn't accept her at first, "Not until I could burp my way through the alphabet." Knowing as we do the realities of the backstage world, she was probably only half-joking.

Before the intense partnership began, one of the issues that Joanie had to resolve for herself when she and Levesque first discussed bringing her into the fold was, "Could I handle living on the road?" Levesque already had the rigorous experience of doing so, and needed to make sure that Joanie was ready for the pressure of touring. Not everyone can stand a life spent occupying endless strange hotels and never eating a meal cooked in one's own kitchen. But Laurer was more than ready; this was what she had been waiting for all of her life.

However, there was a surprise ahead, for on that initial tour, she got more than she bargained for. In addition to the bumps and bruises that she was picking up, her heart was also under attack. She and Levesque were falling in love. "By the end of the tour," Laurer said, "we did the big kiss."

The hardest part of the tour was keeping the other wrestlers from picking up on the fact that their relationship was more than just a professional business partnership. "I didn't want people to think that she didn't pay her dues," Levesque said, "that she was only in the World Wrestling Federation because I wanted a girlfriend on the road." They knew they wouldn't be able to keep their secret forever. How they ever managed to find the time to fall in love is another matter entirely. Because of their size and fame, the typical romantic candlelit dinners were impossible. Both wrestlers have indicated that they can't even go out in public together without someone recognizing them and wanting to interrupt them to talk about wrestling.

But as time went on, they finally had to put an end to secrets and admit to others what they had discovered about each other.

"Paul is not like any boyfriend I've ever known," Chyna has said. "Other guys were intimidated by me because I was so big. It was like their machismo was threatened. But it was never a problem with Paul. He makes me feel like the ultimate woman because he's a real man."

Luckily for us, their behind-the-scenes friendship transformed well into solid ring chemistry

before the fans and the cameras, and its growth has been a joy to behold.

Michael Lano, the wrestling dentist, has a unique perspective on their relationship, based on his over thirty years of watching wrestlers up close and personal behind the scenes. The wrestling life is not an easy one to endure, and he explains why Joanie has turned out to be more stable than many another grappler. "But in her case what makes it a lot easier," he shared, "and I'm getting a little serious here, [is that with] the male wrestlers, it's fairly common for them to cheat on their wives and all of that. They get very lonely when they're not around their families. But with Hunter and Chyna, they're their own family, and they are the most well-adjusted couple I've seen in a long time in wrestling. There are many couples in wrestling that either break up, split apart, do drugs and all of that, and they are the cleanest, most wholesome couple in all of wrestling that I've ever seen." So the verdict is in—not only have Chyna and Triple H been good for us the audience, but they've been good for each other as well.

Together, they form a mutual admiration society as never before seen in the ring.

"The world has never seen an athlete like her," Levesque has said of Laurer. "And I can guarantee that no one ever will."

In return, Joanie has stated many a time, "He makes me feel like the ultimate woman because he's a real man."

It's no wonder that this pair is so perfect for each other. In an interview with the staff at *Inside Wrestling*, Chyna indicated that what she admires most in a man is the ability to accept her as an equal, which makes it understandable that she and Triple H would get together. He is not intimidated by her, because he is strong enough to be her equal.

Almost.

The two are so closely seen as a seamless team that they often make public appearances, touring together to promote the fun side of wrestling. One of their recent spots was when Triple H and Chyna appeared on *The Martin Short Show* on November 12, 1999.

For most of their early time together, Chyna had often been a spoiler in the shadow of Triple H, rather than a brawler in her own right. She has changed the course of more Triple H bouts than can be counted. One such example was at SummerSlam 1998, when Chyna interfered in a Ladder match between the Rock and Triple H, delivering a low blow to Hunter's opponent, as had been her trademark. The wrestler known as

People's Champion, the Rock, had complained about this situation. Rocky Mavia had said that "Hunter Hearst Helmsley has never beaten the Rock fair and square even once, and as long as that genetic freak Chyna is around, the Rock is never going to get a fair chance at kicking his butt."

But Joanie thinks that the Rock, and any other wrestler who thinks that she may have ruined the direction of their bouts, had better think again. "He's a man, a real man, and the best damn wrestler in the federation," she has said of partner Hunter. She insists that rather than making things unfair for the competition, she only gets involved to make things fair again for Hunter. "The only times I have to help him out is when he's getting cheated, which happens all the time. I never really know what he's going to do next, but whatever it is, I'll be by his side."

Paul Levesque heartily concurs. "Wherever Chyna goes, I go," he has said. "She is the most amazing woman ever created by God."

Other wrestlers, such as Mark Henry, the former Olympian known as Sexual Chocolate, have felt the same way, too. Henry has said that "Only I can bring out the true woman in Chyna."

But he is careful not to repeat such outlandish claims around Helmsley.

When Triple H was asked in the summer of '99 what was the luckiest thing that ever happened to him in his long and varied lifetime, he had two words, and they weren't the ones that you've come to expect from his affiliation with D-X. They were, very reasonably, "Meeting Chyna."

That was probably the luckiest thing that ever happened to us wrestling fans as well.

# CHAPTER 6

# CHYNA DOLL

Asking what this gorgeous grapplerette does to relax during her time out of the ring is almost a foolish question, because when is she ever far from a bout? There's hardly time for rest and relaxation, considering that in addition to being on the road over 280 days per year, she must commit to a grueling exercise schedule of four days a week in the gym, with two punishing hours per day of strenuous exercise.

Most of us would crumble under that sort of stress, regardless of the personal rewards. To keep going day after day with that demanding lifestyle, Joanie always managed to maintain her endless sense of humor, which carried her through life long before there was a Chyna, and offstage she has always made those around her laugh. She cracks jokes and chews gum, reacting to her troubles from the very beginning with outrageous puns.

First of all, forget the all-consuming national pastime of Nintendo and PlayStation. No blisters on her thumbs for Chyna. Those pursuits are far too tame for a woman who spends her days and nights tossing men about the ring like matchsticks. "I hate video games," she has said.

Instead, she might kick back with one of her favorite movies, like *Pulp Fiction*, depending on her mood, or any film containing her favorite actor or actress, Arnold Schwarzenegger and Glenn Close. Perhaps if she was in the mood for channel-surfing instead, she might pause to watch one of the TV shows she particularly enjoys, such as *The Simpsons* or *60 Minutes*. (And though she loves the edgy comedy of *The Simpsons* and wishes she could meet the writers of the show, her favorite cartoon character turns out not to be Homer or Bart or even Lisa—no, she sees herself instead as the X-man named Wolverine, the Marvel comics character with retractable adamantium claws and a growling, no-nonsense attitude.) She might listen to a Van Halen CD, but she's been mum so far on whether she goes for the Sammy Haggar or David Lee Roth incarnation of the band. If a guess had to be made, it would perhaps be the latter, as she's been known to swoon for men in spandex.

Michael Lano

When Joanie
Laurer wrestled
as Joanie Lee

Michael Lano

**D**on't piss off the Ninth Wonder of the World!

**F**ormidable even when out of the ring

Jeff Eisenberg

**The fans love Joanie!**

**Red, white, and blue. Do you recognize this woman?**

Michael Lano

Sue Schneider

**T**urning heads at the Emmy Awards

Paul Fenton

**W**ith boyfriend Paul Levesque, aka Triple H

Tom Miller

# Warrior Queen

**T**he champion!

Jeff Eisenberg

Tom Miller

**T**he new sidekick, Miss Kitty

Tough but sexy

Albert L. Ortegg

Looking beautiful at the
American Comedy Awards

She likes to knit, but it is doubtful that she's the one responsible for all of those tight-fitting outfits that she wears in the ring, seeming more a vinyl and leather kind of girl.

She loves riding roller coasters, and was particularly enamored with the *Twilight Zone* Tower of Terror ride at Disney World. She was once given a special tour of the attraction after a taping of *Live with Regis & Kathy Lee*. For those who haven't made it to Florida, this is not your traditional ride. The Tower of Terror's thrills are all vertical. After being strapped into an antique elevator car, you are lifted up thirteen stories and then dropped back down the elevator shaft in free fall. Shrieking like the rest of us, the warrior queen was as thrilled as a little kid. In fact, she was so taken with the ride that even though she was being mobbed by fans, she rode it repeatedly, almost missing her flight home. No wonder that the Ninth Wonder of the World loves roller coasters, as her life has been something of a roller coaster itself!

Aside from the time spent with Paul Levesque, that's about it for Joanie Laurer. Over the years, the The Ninth Wonder of the World has learned that the public life is a lonely life, and that one of the main things missing is time for herself.

"I'm not never Chyna," she said on a *MegaStar*

Internet chat. "It's twenty-four hours a day work."

And you know something? We bet she wouldn't change it for anything.

# CHAPTER 7

# FEUDS AND BETRAYALS

Chyna has become embroiled in many feuds within her short time in the World Wrestling Federation. But considering the nature of the antic-ridden beast, anything else would have been extremely unlikely. It is probably impossible for any wrestler to last more than a few bouts before dramatic allegiances and rivalries begin. The convoluted plots of the wrestling world undoubtedly exist to give soap operas something to seem stable by comparison.

One of the strangest run-ins Chyna ever had was with Mark Henry, the six-foot-one, 385-pound former Olympic weightlifter and self-proclaimed "Strongest Man in the World," who is known more familiarly to wrestling audiences as Sexual Chocolate. This ebony titan from Silsbee, Texas, debuted with the WWF in September 1996, trouncing Jerry Lawler (whose girlfriend, as will be seen in a later chapter, is Chyna's newest side-kick Miss Kitty, continuing the Joanie Laurer connection). The reason this particular feud was so odd is that it was one of the rare ones based on love rather than hate. Henry considered himself a lover rather than a fighter, even though with his massive bulk he could be quite devastating in the ring. He was often battening on one female ring personality or another, and for a period of time a weekly subplot was his search for a therapist who could help him with his sexual addiction.

Of course, given enough time, the world's greatest lover and the ring's greatest specimen of womanhood eventually found each other. Henry decided that he was in love with Chyna, and would accept no substitutes. He began writing romantic poetry for her, which was terribly embarrassing to her when read on the air—and due to its ragged rhymes, should have been embarrassing to him, had he not been so smitten. He once actually convinced Chyna to go on a date with him, but that was obtained only through subterfuge. He earned the assignation as pay-ment—that was the only way he would agree to drop a sexual harassment suit that—of all things—he had filed against her.

At the time, Henry happily admitted that Chyna is "the best thing that ever happened to me. She gave my life new meaning."

Luckily for Chyna, Henry's amorous attentions have now turned elsewhere, to the ever-vivacious Mae Young, the eighty-three-year-old grappler still messing it up in the ring long after others would have retired. Henry, who had once claimed that "Chyna and I are gonna be together forever," is as fickle as ever, for the latest subplot has him being Young's protector with a curious tenderness. Octogenarian Young recently took the wrestling world by surprise when she made the announcement that she was pregnant by Henry. The packed auditorium groaned in dismay, and Henry's fellow wrestlers seemed outright disgusted, but standing beside his new love, Sexual Chocolate just beamed. If this claim turns out to be true, and not yet another of Vince McMahon's many publicity stunts, then Young will soon have to be added to the list with which we started this book, and call her the Tenth Wonder of the World.

Henry's role as a thorn in Chyna's side was soon supplanted by Jeff Jarrett, the guitar-swinging chauvinist who resented Chyna's very existence in the field he wanted to claim for men only. This honky-tonk hell-raiser claimed, with very little evidence to be the world's greatest country singer. He had usually used his guitar not for singing, but as a weapon to wham down on the head of many an unsuspecting opponent in a dramatic finishing move—usually when his (or her) back is turned. He's been in the business since he started as a referee at the age of nineteen—though with Jarrett's temper, he couldn't bear to stay on the sidelines for long. (Though it can hardly be said that the wrestling refs, who contrive artfully to somehow always look away just as the most dastardly deeds are done, so they won't have to call the fight, are on the sidelines.) In 1986 Jarrett faced Tony Faulk, defeating him in his first pro match. With partner Billy Travis, with whom he formed the tag team of the Sheepherders, he won the CWA Southern Tag Team title. He made his first appearance in the WWF in 1992, challenging Bret Hart for the Intercontinental Championship, but it wasn't long before he was over in the WCW, winning the U.S. Heavyweight title from Dean Malenko. But the WWF came calling again, and perhaps that was the place he had to be, for this belittler of women needed a worthy target to knock down—and where would he find that biggest female target but in Chyna?

He absolutely hated women wrestlers, and even women audience members. During his final pay-per-view before jumping ship yet again to return to the WCW (that Jarrett must be dizzy by now), he entered the arena with a bag of dirt and a vacuum cleaner, and forced an innocent female audience member, who was only looking forward to a night of rasslin' entertainment, to clean up the ring. No friend to Gloria Steinem, Jarrett further raised Chyna's ire by insulting two of the greatest females ever to trod the canvas, the Fabulous Moolah (who made her wrestling debut in 1949) and Mae Young (who has been wrestling professionally since an unbelievable 1940!). To bring further dishonor on the women's division, he orchestrated the WWF's first mud-wrestling match between his new valet, Miss Kitty, and Ivory.

Chyna captured the Intercontinental title from Jeff Jarrett on October 17, 1999 at the No Mercy pay-per-view, right before he left for the WCW to debut the following night, chased out of the WWF by the Ninth Wonder of the World.

The void of enemy for our fighting female has been filled by the self-styled "Ayatollah of Rock and Rollah" Chris Jericho, also known as Y2J, though that name will surely begin to have less resonance as we move further and further from December 31, 1999. A new nickname is warranted for this wonder boy who at age thirty has already fought his 1,000th career match. The intended career for this young man at age nineteen was journalism, and if he had not been seduced by the wrestling bug and gone off to train at Stu Hart's Wrestling Dungeon, he might very well have been writing this book. Instead, he made his pro wrestling debut on October 2, 1990. As appropriate for a competitor oozing testosterone, he has been involved in many gender-bending stunts, including the time he battled former Triple H tag-team partner Perry Saturn, with the stakes being that the loser was forced to wear a dress—and after winning Jericho kept up the pressure, forcing his opponent to keep wearing that dress for months afterward. Jericho, who recently began writing a music column for *Metal Edge* magazine, may very well write the book on Chyna within the ring.

Facing off against Jericho during the Survivors Series, Chyna made another bit of wrestling history when she became the first wrestler—male or female—to ever perform the Pedigree finishing move when delivered from the top rope.

But the most remarkable and unexpected enemy created by Joanie Laurer over the years was her own boyfriend Paul Levesque, when a plot was devised for Triple H to have the improbable misfortune to land on the wrong side of Chyna. What an odd life it must be for two such close friends to wear one face in front of the public and another behind closed doors. But that is what Laurer has been able to do, and do it well, for the length of her career. The purported division between soulmates was played out on February 15 in an arena in Phoenix, Arizona. The atmosphere in the WWF had been rocky for quite a while. The storyline had miscommunications put Triple H and Chyna on the outs with the Undertaker and his dark sidekicks, and here was where it was all planned to come to a head. It happened when it was least expected, while Helmsley was fighting the Rock in an "I Quit" match. All seemed fine for Triple H, and after the choreographed clash of titans left him clearly in the lead, he finally had the Brahma Bull cowed into submission atop the announcer's table, which often does not last in one piece through the night. Just as Triple H was about to deliver his devastating finishing move, the Pedigree, and had the Rock bent over, arms pinned behind his back, the demonic Kane changed the tide of the night by dominating and grabbing Chyna, the woman Levesque loved, by the throat. The Big Red Machine hefted her into the air, massive fingers crushing her windpipe. Her legs dangled helplessly in a pitiful scene.

At the moment of what should have been his greatest triumph, on the verge of shattering his bitterest enemy, Triple H was faced with a trade—the Rock for Chyna. For anyone who knows the deep real-life relationship between the two, it was truly no choice at all. Levesque was forced to let go of the Rock and the WWF title both, uttering the two most horrible words a wrestler can say in order to save the woman he loved. "I quit" rumbled from his lips in a low deep-throated growl.

But Kane's strength was terrifying, and as Levesque played it, Triple H feared that Chyna might not be able to recover from the onslaught. Triple H had let go of his opponent, and turned his attention now only on Chyna. Was she still the same woman? Would she be able to recover? Triple H had played the role of white knight to rescue his princess, but at this point he did not know whether the princess would be able to care.

He rushed to her side, where she was bent over, attempting to catch her breath. He looked away momentarily, to make sure that their enemies were at bay. And in those seconds one of the greatest betrayals in the history of wrestling was played out. As soon as his back was turned, she struck him with a low blow, clenched fist slamming up powerfully between his legs. The expression on his face at that point, as he sank to his knees, is enough to tell us that we should forget Tom Hanks and Robert DeNiro. If there's ever a category of Academy Award given out for wrestling actors, Paul Levesque should cop the prize. The anguish we were able to read on his face was infectious. We believed that he was tortured both physically and emotionally to realize that Chyna had gone over to the side of his hated enemy Vince McMahon, and we felt that anguish with him. A relationship that had lasted since the early days of Killer Kowalski's school was over. The cords of friendship had been severed.

The audience was stunned, struggling to understand. Chyna explained the reasons behind the rebellion, and the answer wasn't a pretty one. She said that she was tired of carrying the team of D-X all these years. Two years of standing on the sidelines was enough. She felt that she did nothing more than watch as they got all the glory. So she had turned her back on her teammates and had new partners now. In what had to be a wrestling fan's worst nightmare, she embraced corporate honcho Vince McMahon, D-X's most hated adversary. The owner hugged her tightly, his face as ecstatic as Levesque's was devastated.

"It's all about the mighty buck, fellas," she confessed from the ring, explaining the allure of working for Team Corporate for those who just didn't get it, "and the buck stops here." She was often seen to be palling around with Vince and son Shane, who was now taking on a more active, on-screen role in the business, and in whose future career Chyna would now start taking an interest, instead doing for him what she had done so long for Triple H.

The fans were justifiably horrified. Over the next few weeks, as they showed up in arenas across the country to express their opinions on handmade signs, some quite intricate, so that at times it seemed to the wrestlers that there was no audience, only a sea of signs, the angry messages blared out in Magic Marker and cardboard. Chyna's actions had become a major area of concern for wrestling's great subconscious.

WHY, CHYNA, WHY? read one sign.

CHYNA, YOU BROKE MY HEART read another, speaking not just for Triple H, but for all wrestling fans.

And one sign went to the heart of the matter, using the well-known D-Generation-X battle cry against the woman who had so often screamed it the loudest. It read simply, CHYNA, SUCK IT.

The sting of that betrayal was uppermost in Triple H's mind, and he expressed it often, even as he went on with the business of his career. "Hope you can buy a new conscience with that money," he told her later. His anger was so great that he now found himself in the situation of calling his former soulmate a whore.

The other members of D-X were also forceful in their opinions. Badd Ass Billy Gunn, when asked in the pages of the June 1999 issue of *The Wrestler* about the defection of Chyna from D-Generation-X, had nothing good to say about the leather-clad grappler who was once one of his closest friends: "Who the hell cares about her? She double-crossed Triple H, and that means we don't need her anymore. He'll take care of her. She gave up the best thing she ever had, going over to join McMahon's Corporation. We'll get over that. It ain't no big deal. And if Chyna wants to come back, well, then she'd better look somewhere else, because we're not having her."

But things got worse, for not only did Chyna express no interest in returning to the fold, she instead expressed interest only in kicking Helmsley's butt. The site of that kicking was the Pyramid in Memphis, Tennessee. It was perhaps only fitting that the Ninth Wonder of the World should do battle within one of the first Seven. The pay-per-view event was called Valentine's Day Massacre, and would feature a tag-team match-up pitting Chyna and Kane vs. X-Pac and Triple H. There would be no candy and flowers exchanged between the former sweethearts at this event. All that either of them were interested in delivering was pain. As Chyna made her threats, she mocked the holiday.

"Happy Valentine's Day, sweetheart," she said, threatening a trouncing with a sneer that could have rivaled Triple H's own.

Former friends X-Pac and Kane were no slouches, but the spotlight was not on them. The attention of the audience was on Chyna and Triple H.

Once in the ring, Chyna took off her outer shirt and quickly tossed it to one side, immediately ready to rumble. Triple H made an even more dramatic gesture. He removed his own shirt to reveal a tank top with his former partner's name on it. His meaty hands grabbed it at the collar, and he ripped it with an angry gesture. The cloth shredded easily, dividing her name down the middle, his own slap in the face as payback for what Chyna had done, but also a promise and premonition of what he would do to her that very night. He didn't discard the cloth to one side as Chyna did, but instead tossed the pieces in her face. Her face was impassive. She seemed not to react. She would not let her former partner see that she had any doubts about the path they were taking.

When the action began, the participants played out the match so as to ensure the greatest tension.

The audience knew what it would mean when, on that February night, they would be given the biggest box of candy in wrestling, for they would witness the first time in history that a woman had ever been involved legitimately in a match. As Chyna, Joanie had gotten involved as bodyguard to play with the odds on behalf of Triple H or the rest of D-X, but this was history in the making.

"Chyna was always the bigger star than Triple H," squealed Jerry "the King" Lawler at ringside. "She made Triple H what he was."

It was more than that, it was a reciprocal relationship where each made the other look good, but the time for helping each other was past. Now the gloves were off, and the audience waited for the real center of attraction, when the two former partners faced off.

But at first it looked as if it would never get that far, and the debacle the audience was hoping for would never arrive. Chyna fought X-Pac, and Triple H fought Kane, but somehow, as each tag took place, Laurer and Levesque avoided being in the ring together. But when they were, the kudos went to Chyna, for she covered her boyfriend for a pin, albeit with a little help from Kane.

Chyna defeated Triple H, and Joanie Laurer, the girl who hated to part with her Winnie the

Pooh dolls, had defeated wrestling's stereotypes. For the first time in the history of the sport, a woman had taken on a man as part of a tag team, and with a little help from her friends—which is how things usually go in the convoluted world of wrestling—she'd come out the other side triumphant.

Before the tides of the evening could change, Kane pulled Chyna away, getting her out of the ring and away from her awakening opponent. They walked out as a team, a new force to be reckoned with. Chyna was staggering but happy as she was helped along by her new partner, Kane, with whom she would rise to new heights in the WWF.

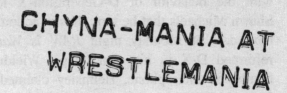

# CHYNA-MANIA AT WRESTLEMANIA

WrestleMania was one of Vince McMahon's most brilliant brainchildren, in a career that has known many of them. He brought together the biggest and the best of an annual match-up of the fan's most eagerly desired bouts, carefully directing all plotlines toward this event. The first WrestleMania, back in 1985, brought in a new age of wrestling popularity, with mainstream stars such as Cyndi Lauper, Muhammad Ali, and Liberace in attendance. The third broke live attendance records. For a decade and a half WrestleMania has been the Indy 500, the Super Bowl, and World Series rolled into one, the pinnacle of wrestling achievement. Momentous events always occur at, around, or slightly before WrestleMania.

History is usually made, and as WrestleMania XV approached, Chyna was looking forward to making some further history of her own.

At WrestleMania XIV the previous year, on March 30, 1998, Triple H became so disgusted with the behavior of D-Generation-X leader Shawn Michaels that he took drastic action. The next day, at Monday night *RAW is War*, he reformed D-X in his own image. Wielding a bombastic microphone, Helmsley claimed that Shawn Michaels had dropped the ball, and he was therefore taking over leadership of D-X himself, adding X-Pac to the lineup.

Helmsley was slated to be at the center of attention at this year's WrestleMania as well. He was due to face Kane for the title, in a rivalry that is longstanding. Helmsley was still angry that Chyna had formed a bond with Kane. Their battles had been going on ever since. And recently, Kane had turned to using more than just his fists to fight his new archrival.

Three weeks prior to WrestleMania, Kane had even sent a fireball hurling at Helmsley. Triple H was fast though, and the blast meant for him exploded instead in Chyna's eyes. The normally unfeeling Kane, in an unusually tender gesture for him, picked her up, cradled her in his arms, and took her out of the arena. Triple H watched Kane walk off with the woman who should've been his, feeling somewhat to blame.

The strange relationship continued a week earlier, when the odd form of Goldust appeared in the ring in his long flowing robes and painted face. Kane did not know what to make of this, and then, at the last moment it was revealed that under the makeup was not the man called Goldust, but instead Triple H, hiding in the outrageous getup of the same wrestler he had fought when Chyna first debuted. The reason for the long robes was so Triple H could bring in a weapon of his own, since Kane had escalated the battle. Triple H fireballed him with a bazooka, and the other wrestler burst into flame.

This was hell on earth for the character called Kane, whose storyline had it that his face had been disfigured by fire as a child. That face is constantly covered by a mask, as is his scarred body by a devil-red suit. The 326-pound, seven-foot-tall behemoth was forced to relive that childhood trauma when hit by Triple H's firebomb. Now, the Undertaker's brother had even more reason to wish to crush Triple H.

So by the time that Sunday, March 29, 1999, came around, there was more than enough hate to go around at WrestleMania XV.

The First Union Center States Arena in Philadelphia, Pennsylvania, was packed, as is the norm for WrestleMania events. Tickets were hard to come by, as they never went on sale to the general public. In another unique McMahon strategy, they sold out by mail-order request alone. The scalpers were having a field day, if they could get any product to push. The fighter Joanie Laurer had created had quite a hand in the events that were to come. Shane McMahon, son of the boss, was to defend the European title against X-Pac. But he had not won it cleanly—Chyna had helped put that belt around his waist in much the same way that she had formerly helped Triple H claw his way to the top. The McMahons were learning that Team Corporate's dollars had been well spent. Chyna would always deliver as promised.

Chyna had given Shane the European Championship title by sticking herself into a match at *RAW is War*. Shane had been taking a terrible beating in his fight with X-Pac. X-Pac was taking it personally, feeling that he had to show that a kid from the mean streets could sock it to someone born with wrestling's silver spoon in his mouth. It looked as if, left to his own devices, Shane would fail. But then fate intervened in the form of a warrior queen. While Shane was down and about to be beaten senseless, Chyna handed him the heavy championship belt and helped him to his feet. Shane used that belt to brutally beat X-Pac. Shane, barely able to stand, fell unconscious atop a downed X-Pac. Chyna, in a further bit of subterfuge, slipped the belt from the ring before the ref could notice and declare a disqualification. Shane was declared the winner, which meant that he won the right to go to WrestleMania. His confidence was up, knowing that Chyna would help him there as well.

The scheduling of the night had it that before Shane and X-Pac would face off again, Triple H and Kane would first have at each other. But the wild card in both these matches, Triple H vs. Kane, and Shane McMahon vs. X-Pac, was Chyna.

Kane entered the arena in one of the weirder sets of circumstances for the start of a professional match. As he came down the runway and neared the ring, he was savagely attacked—only it wasn't a well-muscled opponent looking to give a boost to his enemy. Instead, he was beaten up by a man in a chicken suit, much the same kind that's worn by a baseball team mascot.

Because of Triple H's previous use of a disguise, Kane was worried that it might be an old enemy once again attacking him, and about to pull out a hidden weapon. So Kane began hammering on the feathered opponent, who did not defend himself well, whether due to lack of skills or simply the ungainly suit. But when the large chicken mask fell off, it was revealed that the chicken hadn't been his opponent in disguise. In an odd confluence of sports and wrestling, it was instead Pete Rose, the legendary baseball player who left that sport under a cloud. Kane, disgusted, wanted to get the main event going, so he quickly tombstoned Rose, who was taken away while Kane's traditional fireworks blasted and his creepy organ music played.

Beneath his signature red lights, Kane waited for his opponent. He carefully studied the runway, watching as the chicken-suited Rose was escorted away. But it turned out that he was too intent on watching, for as the signature music of Triple H began, Helmsley did not come down the runway as expected. Instead, Triple H surged from the crowd on the opposite side of the arena. He climbed into the ring at Kane's back and formed a mighty fist to attack with a low blow in a sneaky move before Kane was ready.

As strange as it seems, this too was thanks to Chyna. She was affecting the match without even being present, for without Chyna to help him, Triple H obviously felt he had to do something devious in order to survive.

Triple H, in black and silver tights and a black and green tank top, attacked furiously, showing great anger at the man who stole his partner. This was no longer business. Some matches are impersonal, with opponents who hold no grudge against each other, but the best ones grow out of deep resentments. And Chyna was the cause of Triple H's resentment now.

Levesque was a fierce warrior that night, and planted Kane on the mat, but in his moment of possible triumph, Chyna chose to reenter the equation. More like a hurricane than a woman, she came striding down the walkway in a silver-spangled bikini. Her determination was so clear, so overpowering, that things looked bad for Triple H. Her hard face was void of emotion as she strode toward the ring, presumably there to help her fallen Kane. The fans were angry, shouting at the way the odds had abruptly changed, and Triple H was angrier than all the fans put together.

The crowd held its collective breath as it wondered whether the woman warrior had arrived to merely gloat or to take an active hand in the destruction of her former close friend. Even as cheerleader she could hurt Triple H, but if she chose to throw her brawn against him, he would not have a chance in hell against Kane.

Her action was so shocking that *Pro Wrestling Illustrated* would rate it as one of the top five minutes of WrestleMania XV.

Chyna entered the ring with a metal chair, as if about to use it on her former partner, but instead, took out Kane.

Chyna was back. The Ninth Wonder of the World had returned to D-Generation-X, turning her back on the McMahons, Team Corporate, and the big bucks that had enticed her. Loyalty and friendship had won out over the paycheck.

The crowd cheered wildly at the sight they never expected to see.

Chyna ran at Triple H and leaped into his arms. She held him tightly, and he walked around the ring with one arm held high into the air and the other around the prize worth more to him than any belt—Chyna and her affection. As he carried her about the ring, Chyna raised a hand and pumped it in the air, exulting in their reunion.

Triple H was exhausted, but triumphant as never before. The crowd roared its approval. D-X was back together again, and they all knew what that meant—more danger ahead. More thrills, chills, and excitement.

"The worst day in my life was the day I saw Chyna go over to the opposite side and become my enemy," Levesque later said. "I think she felt the same way."

This double cross of Kane put an odd twist on

the rest of the events planned for that night. Shane McMahon, son of the owner—who was scheduled to be the guest referee for the main event of the night, the Rock's battle with Steve Austin—had to defend a title that he needed Chyna's help to win before she left, abandoning him and Team Corporate.

Backstage, with all the members of D-X seemingly one happy family again, X-Pac appeared even more confident that he would regain his stolen title from McMahon. As Badd Ass Billy Gunn, Road Dogg Jesse James, Chyna, and X-Pac listened with glee, Triple H declared that "Chyna has come home, and D-X is one big house again, stronger than it's ever been. D-X is whole, and there ain't nothing stronger."

The 229-pound Shane McMahon entered, full of bravado. He was accompanied by fellow wrestler Test. (Test was eventually to marry Stephanie McMahon, before Triple H sent things awry.) He seemed confident, even without Chyna at his side.

But the confidence did not last long, for after a match full of tricks and treachery, the 204-pound X-Pac was about to win. That's when Chyna and Triple H reentered the arena. X-Pac was happy to see his pals, and glad that they were there to see him retake the belt and start the celebration early.

But instead of rejoicing in the impending win, Triple H attacked the stunned X-Pac. While Chyna distracted the ref so he'd miss the goings-on in the ring, Triple H turned the tide of the bout, dragging Shane over on top of X-Pac. Once Chyna let the ref get back to the doings in the ring, he quickly declared that Shane had retained the title. The announcers were confused by this double cross, and so was the crowd, as Triple H took the opportunity to knock down X-Pac once again. All of the night's early activities were a ruse to hide the fact that it wasn't Chyna who went back to the side of Triple H to rejoin D-X, but rather Triple H who had jumped ship to now side with Team Corporate.

"Chyna and I were meant to be together," he said, "and Vince McMahon made us an offer we couldn't refuse."

Later on, Hunter Hearst Helmsley explained the machinations behind it all, and why they handled the night the way they did. "Hell, when she got in good with the corporation, she had to convince Vince McMahon that I could be trusted, and then they brought me in. I had no second thoughts, but I didn't want to leave without making a huge impact on D-X."

As for the rest of D-X, Badd Ass Billy Gunn and Road Dogg Jesse James were outraged that night, and charged the ring to attack. While Chyna cradled and protected Shane, Test and Triple H together took care of the New Age Outlaws, destroying them for the night.

"Everything went perfectly, just according to plan" Triple H later told reporters. "Nobody knew what hit them. But now the corporation is stronger than ever."

On *Live with Regis & Kathy Lee*, Joanie once said, "Win if you can. Lose if you must. But always cheat!" Yet somehow, even when pulling shenanigans like she did that night at WrestleMania, we don't feel cheated, and she still manages to keep our respect.

# CHAPTER 9

# CHYNA GETS READY TO RUMBLE

On January 14, 1999, at Arrowhead Pond in Anaheim California, Chyna made history by becoming the first woman ever to enter the mass mayhem that is the Royal Rumble. This participation was the realization of a dream, particularly because Chyna has never bothered to wrestle in the women's division, feeling that the challenges there were not sufficient to her dreams. She hopes to someday become the WWF Champion, reigning over all genders, and the Royal Rumble was the first step toward her goal. What better way to prove herself than to measure her talents against all of the WWF's best and brightest?

What is the Royal Rumble? One might as well try to describe a riot. It is perhaps Vince McMahon's most ingenious way of giving the audience what they want. Instead of sending two men into the ring to compete head-to-head for a championship, why not send in thirty, with the possibility that all of them might remain standing to get into one gigantic brawl? There is strength in numbers, but there are ratings and dollars as well. So what McMahon dreamed up was a match in which a new wrestler must enter the ring every two minutes in an order determined by lottery. The way that wrestlers get those numbers in the lottery is often subject to outside interference.

To be eliminated from the competition, a wrestler must be put over the top rope by another. If a wrestler chooses to go under the ropes to attack another, he—or she, as is the case with Chyna, and only Chyna—is still in the game. Obviously, a wrestler chosen to be number one has a tough ride to the top; he must survive where twenty-nine other wrestlers have failed. The luckiest wrestler comes in at number thirty, beginning the bout an hour fresher than the first entrant. The first of these spectacular Royal Rumbles was held in 1988, and was won by "Hacksaw" Jim Duggan.

In 1999 Steve Austin, the Texas Rattlesnake, was the man to beat. He was also the man everyone *wanted* to beat. Vince McMahon hated Austin with a passion, and in order to make sure that his wrestlers felt that passion too, he not only rigged the event so that Austin was number one, he also put a bounty of $100,000 on his head.

Interviewed before the rumble began, the members of D-X discussed whether their loyalties would survive in the ring, when each knew that one of the other D-X members might have to be eliminated.

"It goes like this," Triple H said. "D-X is as tight as anybody can be, but it's for the WWF title. It's for $100,000. It's every man for himself."

But then Chyna leaned into the microphone and uttered the two magic words that made it clear to fans of true women's wrestling that she gave way to no one. To Helmsley's "every man," she appended:

"And woman!"

The order of the wrestlers entering the rumble was as follows:

1. Steve Austin
2. Vince McMahon
3. Golga
4. Droz
5. Edge
6. Gillberg
7. Steve Blackman
8. Dan Severn
9. Tiger Ali Singh

10. Blue Meanie
11. Mable
12. Road Dog
13. Gangrel
14. Kurrgan
15. Al Snow
16. Goldust
17. Godfather
18. Kane
19. Ken Shamrock
20. Billy Gunn
21. Test
22. Big Bossman
23. Triple H
24. Val Venis
25. X-Pac
26. Mark Henry
27. Jeff Jarrett
28. D-Lo Brown
29. Owen Hart
30. Chyna

In order to earn this favored final spot, Chyna had to be declared the winner of the Corporate Royal Rumble, held between the members of D-Generation-X and Team Corporate. In order to get the berth, she had the pleasure of eliminating Vince McMahon himself.

It was a thrilling match from the very beginning. The feud between Austin and McMahon spilled out of the ring and around the arena, including the women's bathroom. Their tussle seemed to end with Austin being set upon by McMahon's goons, who overpowered him and sent him on a trip to the hospital. (Austin returned later in a commandeered ambulance to whip McMahon's butt.) Things only heated up from there.

Ninety minutes in, history was made. After all of the other wrestlers had worn themselves ragged, Chyna entered the ring as the thirtieth entrant. The first woman to ever enter a Royal Rumble headed straight for Sexual Chocolate Mark Henry, and took him out of the competition. Perhaps she should have paid less attention to getting even for old feuds, and more attention to the most dangerous man of the night. She was so pleased to have settled an old score with this elimination that she jeered Henry rather than watching her back.

Stone Cold Steve Austin, who was well aware that he had a $100,000 prize on his head, and knew that Chyna was a tough contender, particularly in her rested condition, snuck up on her and clotheslined her out of the ring before she had a chance to collect the money. If she had to be eliminated, perhaps it should be taken as a compliment that it was Steve Austin, currently the most feared male contender in wrestling, who did it.

The eventual winner of this latest thirty person rampage was Vince McMahon, but the cause of women in wrestling was the true winner.

# CHAPTER 10

# QUEEN OF THE RING

On June 27, 1999, Joanie Laurer would once again take the warrior called Chyna to new heights of wrestling history. Inside the Greensboro Coliseum in Greensboro, North Carolina, 21,108 hard-core wrestling fans gathered to see who would be crowned the 1999 King of the Ring. For as long as the King of the Ring title had been contested, nothing as decidedly different as this had occurred before, and the fans knew it.

That year, the rest of the wrestlers would have to contend with Chyna.

For the first time ever, a woman was being given the chance to compete and perhaps become the Queen of the Ring. There was some controversy surrounding Chyna's role, as there always is when a woman attempts to go where only men have been before. Many thought that Triple H, who was guaranteed a berth in 1999 because of his previous year's win, should not have thrown away his slot by giving it to Chyna. They felt he deserved to be there himself because of the previous title win.

Whatever the reason Levesque stepped aside, Joanie Laurer was thankful. What a difference a year makes. At the previous year's King of the Ring superevent in Pittsburgh, she never got a chance to wrestle before the sellout crowd of 17,087. She was there to watch the feats of others, observing, sometimes interfering, but never competing in her own right. Never having a title on the line.

First she stood by and watched X-Pac fight, yet again playing the bodyguard role. She did not speak. Her only expression was a high five given to the former 1-2-3 Kid as he took on Owen Hart. (Hart, who had debuted in June 7, 1996, was sadly to die in the ring in Kansas City, Missouri, on May 23, 1999, in one of wrestling's great tragedies.) As X-Pac's match went on, Chyna was the spoiler again. When Mark Henry hit the ring and slammed X-Pac, Vader entered to slam Henry. With the ref so distracted by the melee outside, Chyna went into the ring to put a DDT on Owen Hart, allowing X-Pac to win and advance to the semifinals in a battle she knew she could just have easily won alone for herself. The match over, she spoke not a word with the man whose back she was guarding. She just put his arm around her shoulder and led him off.

Then, at the next match, she was again almost a mere spectator, as Road Dogg Jesse James and Badd Ass Billy Gunn, the New Age Outlaws, took to the ring. Chyna was once more silent as the D-X duo took on Midnight Express. No wrestling that time either, though she did get a chance to deliver a low blow on the opposing team's manager, James E. Cornette, after he threatened to hit Gunn with a belt.

After a King of the Ring history like that, it's easy to understand why Chyna was itching for some action of her own. And she knew she would get it, particularly coming up against her slated opponent, Road Dogg Jesse James.

Before the matches even began, Chyna staked out her territory. While Jerry Lawler interviewed Road Dogg, Chyna, in a brazen attack, entered the ring to slap her challenger-to-be. Lawler watched helplessly as his segment descended into chaos. Road Dogg's response to this invasion was slow, because regardless of his flaws, he was still the sort of man who had qualms about fighting a woman. He tried to retaliate, but before he could punch her back, Triple H interfered. Dogg punched Triple H instead, knocking him to the mat with a furious blow, but before Dogg could make use of his temporary advantage, Chyna got in a low blow, slamming a fist into that portion of a male's anatomy that is most precious to him. Chyna and Triple H then joined in a vicious two-on-one attack, kicking Road Dogg again and again while he was down. Then, as Triple H pinned back Road Dogg's arms, Chyna delivered a strong right fist to his jaw.

All this before the fight had even begun!

The stage was set. Chyna had thrown down the gauntlet and issued her challenge: *I'm as tough as any man you ever faced, and you'd better get used to it.*

As the night progressed, Chyna seemed unconcerned. She even did color commentary with Triple H, the previous year's King of the Ring winner, as the Rock fought Ken Shamrock. Joanie Laurer got a chance to demonstrate some of her language skills by chatting with the Spanish commentators in their native tongue.

The first of the quarter-final matchups to determine who would get the title match was Hardcore Holly vs. X-Pac. X-Pac won his event through a disqualification after being hit by a chair that Holly ripped from under Howard Finkel, one of the ring announcers. Chyna's adversary that evening, fellow D-X-er Road Dogg Jesse James, had to rush the ring to chase off Holly before that outraged bleached blond could exact his revenge.

Then came the second stage of the King of the Ring competition, the war of the titans, as the towering giant the Big Show brought his 500-pound, seven-foot-two-inch body against Kane, the Undertaker's brother, whose 328-pound frame suddenly looked scrawny by comparison. Things were going well for the Big Show until Hardcore Holly rushed the ring while the referee was unconscious, to seek the only vengeance he could take that night. The Big Show had turned a car over on Holly just the week before, and the blond brawler wanted payback. Kane choke-slammed Holly, then choke-slammed the Big Show as well. Then Kane used the chair that Holly had left behind to knock the Big Show unconscious while the ref was out, so there was no chance of disqualification.

At first it looked as if the third of the quarter-final matches was over before it even began. Badd Ass Billy Gunn brought all of his sculpted 268 pounds to the ring, and his opponent Ken Shamrock, the brawler from San Diego, was not to be seen in the arena. Cameras took the audience backstage, where medics were preparing to cart off Shamrock to the hospital due to the grappler's confrontation with Steve Blackman earlier in the evening. But not even internal bleeding can stop a wrestler from rising to the occasion to become King of the Ring, and when Mr. Ass taunted him from ringside, the 235-pound Shamrock flung the medics aside and rushed to the arena. Better that he had stayed with the doctors, because he would need them again before the night was out. Billy Gunn focused on the Shamrock's injured midsection, capitalizing on his rib injuries. With Shamrock bleeding from the mouth, the referee finally had to end the match.

Where there were six, now there were three. The outcome of the first matches meant that Billy Gunn, Kane, and X-Pac were to move forward to the semifinals. Would Chyna join them, and do battle against X-Pac for the chance to move onto the finals? Though Chyna was the first woman to ever enter the King of the Ring competition, she had no doubt that she had a chance of winning. "When I was a little girl, I only wanted to be a princess," she said. "And now I'm all grown up, and tonight I'm going to be a queen."

Road Dogg entered the ring first with his usual arrogant bravado. Wielding the mike, he raised his hands high over his head and ordered his music to be stopped. "Welcome to the Dogg House," he shouted, as if he owned the night and there was no doubt about the outcome. "If you ain't down with that, I got two words for you—"

He did not have to complete his thought—the fans, primed by his performance, finished the statement:

"Suck it!"

But once the focus turned to his opponent entering the arena, Dogg suddenly seemed nervous, perhaps remembering that before the match, when she was flanked by Triple H, Chyna had only this to say about her competitor-to-be:

"Road Dogg, you've got big brass balls to step in the ring with me."

He'd been raised not to hit a woman, as most men have been, and what he was about to endure went against all his training. He seemed unnerved to take part in one of the most unusual matches the wrestling world had ever known.

The arena went dark, and with green strobe lights flashing and the music blasting, the Ninth Wonder of the World strode down the walkway.

"I've been waiting for this for a long time," Lawler squealed with delight from ringside. The fans had been waiting too. "Let's see it happen!"

The battle that the fans saw was not only between Chyna and Road Dogg, but between Road Dogg and his own conscience. For most of the match, Joanie Laurer seemed to be leading, while Dogg showed a restraint unseen in his other matches. But once the beating that Laurer was giving him sank into his brain, he threw his scruples to the wind, and fought back furiously, even introducing a chain as a weapon, unseen by the ref.

Triple H tried to interfere in her behalf, but Commissioner Shawn Michaels, the ultimate power in the WWF at the time, had Levesque ejected from the arena, and so Joanie did not advance. At least not within the King of the Ring competition.

But she did advance another ring higher on the ladder of history, a little bit closer to what she truly wanted out of her life.

Chyna may have lost, but she showed that she could compete. She forced the wrestlers and fans to admit that she was as good as any of them.

Once Chyna's match was over, the fans turned their attention to the other bouts that night, such as Vince McMahon fighting Stone Cold Steve Austin for control of his company, and the match to determine who would become the 1999 King of the Ring. (It was to be Badd Ass Billy Gunn in a fast and furious win over X-Pac.)

But what Chyna did that June 27, 1999, in Greenboro, North Carolina, was far more important to the future of wrestling, because with her powerful performance she proved that indeed a woman's place was in the ring.

# INTERCONTINENTAL QUEEN

Chyna had other mountains still to climb as she continued her journey to prove that her title of Ninth Wonder of the World was justified. The name of that next mountain was Jeff Jarrett, and it was at the pay-per-view event Unforgiven, on September 26, 1999, at the Charlotte Coliseum in Charlotte, North Carolina, that she was due to scale him. Joanie would fight Jarrett for the Intercontinental Championship belt in an inter-gender bout.

Jarrett was a formidable and obnoxious opponent. He was the WWF's first six-time Intercontinental Champion. No other wrestler had come any closer to that feat than as a four-time champion. Chyna's road to the ring to face him was a devious one. As is always the way for Joanie Laurer, she reached out her hand and grasped her own future.

Jarrett had been foolish enough to seek a contender for the title by posting an open contract for the match on his dressing room door. He would do battle with the first contender willing to sign his name on the bottom of that contract. The operative word here in Jarrett's mind was "man." He surely never expected that while Badd Ass Billy Gunn—having seen the contract and lusting for the shot—was out looking for a pen, Chyna would instead whip one out and boldly affix her name there. Jarrett was insulted and incensed, but he was forced to go through with it and give the warrior woman a shot. He intended to keep his word, but that did not mean he intended to do so honorably.

Recent events had set the stage for an exciting night. On the Thursday night Smackdown that aired before Unforgiven, Chyna came to the defense of a poor stagehand who was being abused by Jarrett. She was in total control that night, hitting him over the head with a frying pan, taking off his pants, and putting them on herself to let him know who really wore the pants in the wrestling world. As he lay knocked out and flat on his back, while Miss Kitty looked on helplessly, Chyna put an apron on him, a frying pan in one hand, and a spoon in the other. There is a load of bad blood between the macho man and the feminist icon.

Jarrett entered the arena joyfully that night. He came out waving a guitar over his head, expecting an easy win. By his side was Miss Kitty, a lanky blond in a revealing silver bodysuit, who had recently come between Jarrett and his faithful valet, Debra. Going in, Jarrett had to be nervous, though his appearance belied that. That he might become the first male to ever lose a title to a woman had to be on his mind. Fear makes a wonderful motivator.

Once Jarrett was in the ring, the lights went out. Chyna's pumping music played, and as she walked into the arena, the ovation was tumultuous. The cheers of the crowd showed that on this night they were overwhelmingly on her side. The strong response was a fitting reward for how far she'd come.

Of course, no one knew how the night would go, particularly considering one all-important glitch. An ongoing referee strike meant that the ref officiating that night would be a scab, and so his rulings were an unknown factor. But as the match began, neither of the contestants gave any hint that they were worried about how this might affect the outcome.

Once the match began, Jarrett seemed determined to brutalize Chyna. He wanted to destroy her for daring to have the ambition to be there.

"A woman can never do that," he shouted at the crowd, right after one particularly damaging move, daring them to contradict him. "Never!"

But Chyna is no easy opponent, and continued to surprise Jarrett with the level of her Ring expertise. Finally, Miss Kitty, sensing that her wrestler might lose, slipped Jarrett his guitar, recognizing that Chyna was too potent an adversary to defeat without resorting to trickery. The ref was unconscious, and so didn't see this illegal move. The crowd did not like this, and booed Jarrett soundly.

This is when all of the investment Joanie Laurer has made in the past and future of women's wrestling paid off.

Suddenly, from their ringside seats, the Fabulous Moolah and Mae Young leaped forward in support of this new generation of woman wrestler who can best the men at their own game. The two senior citizens took turns punching Jarrett, pushing him back and forth between them, battering him senseless. Jarrett responded by acting like the lowest of the low, and clotheslining them both. He kicked them while they were down, perhaps in this moment applying for the trademark of wrestling's ultimate heel. Then he taunted them as they writhed in pain, and kicked them both out of the ring. The audience screamed at him. Outraged, they came to their feet.

At this point, even Debra, Jarrett's formerly loyal valet, got into the act. She stormed the ring, knocking Miss Kitty to the floor and climbing toward Jarrett. Just as Jarrett was about to get Chyna in a successful figure four leglock, Debra—whether angry at what had happened earlier with Miss Kitty, or in defense of the older women—smashed a guitar over Jarrett's head, using his own weapon against him. Her blow was effective, and he was flat on his back staring at the ceiling, helpless to prevent what was to come next.

Chyna, weakened herself, crawled slowly to Jarrett and pinned him for the three count from the now-awakened ref.

The Ninth Wonder of the World was triumphant. And deep inside, Joanie Laurer must have been in wonder at the miracle of it all. Her hand was raised by the ref, but before she could enjoy her win to its fullest, another ref joined the first in the ring and demanded an instant replay be shown on the Titantron screen.

As the events that passed while the ring ref was unconscious were played out, the leader of the scab referees reversed the decision, disqualifying Chyna. The warrior queen began attacking the ref who countered the decision. First she delivered a low blow, then topped it off with the Pedigree.

Jarrett, meanwhile, was still out cold. Even though he could not get to his feet, it was Chyna who walked away the loser. She was disgusted, but at least the audience was clearly on her side.

Throughout the following weeks, Chyna's search for a rematch was a major subplot in the world of the WWF. While Jarrett continued to growl Cro-Magnon sentiments such as, "Women are weak and men are the dominant species," in the weeks before the next PPV event, Chyna continually showed up to force Jarrett to pay whenever he took out his wrath on a woman. Then, on Monday night *RAW*, she issued a challenge: she and Debra against Jarrett and the ref who reversed the decision disqualifying Chyna. If she pinned successfully during that encounter, Chyna announced, she would win the right to meet him again in battle.

"If I pin you in this ring tonight," she said, "I get my rematch at No Mercy for the Intercontinental title. Or maybe you don't have the balls."

Jarrett accepted the challenge, and earned the right for another shot at the Championship. Was there ever any doubt Chyna would have another chance?

Their match was slated for the October 17,

1999, No Mercy pay-per-view at the Gund Arena in Cleveland, Ohio. It would be one of the strangest matches ever. To win the Intercontinental Championship title, Chyna would have to participate in a Good Housekeeping match designed by Jarrett to teach her the true role of a woman. He wanted to beat her in a strange mutant version of a hard-core match, one in which all appliances were fair game and legal to use.

To prove his point, Jarrett made his entrance that night hefting a stainless steel kitchen sink over one shoulder, ready to send a message not only to Chyna, but also to all the other women of the world. Chyna, too, came prepared, entered with a trash can, a broom, and an indomitable sneer. The outside of the ring was scattered with additional household items that would come into play.

Chyna seemed to hold the upper hand at the start of the bout. She began the match in total control, and the fans loved it. This is what they'd come to see. They might not want to see a woman win, but Jarrett had proven himself so obnoxious in recent weeks that they sure didn't want to see him win.

The weapons this pair of grapplers used on each other added up to the strangest arsenal ever to enter the ring. Gleaming trashcans were just the start of it. Heads were bonked with frying pans, a salami, an ironing board, a banana, a fresh fish, whipped cream, tongs, milk, flour and eggs. Chyna even hit him in the face with two pies. But this was not Three Stooges routine—this was for real.

Jarrett's decisive move occurred while a ref was knocked out, as they so often seem to be. He called to Kitty for his belt, which he slammed into Chyna's face, teasing her with what had once seemed so close. Jeff Jarrett pinned Chyna then, and the ref, awake once more, counted out the full three. Jarrett and Miss Kitty were triumphant in retaining the title, and Jarrett's manhood, but there was a special extra twist to the evening.

As the winning duo went up the runway with their prize, they were chased by the ref, who informed them that since the belt was not a household item, it was ruled illegal. Referee Teddy Long reversed the decision and returned to the ring. The ref prepared to restart the match, and commanded the opponents to continue until there was a legal pin.

Jarrett was incensed, so much so that he turned his attention away from his opponent, turning his fury on the ref instead. While he was occupied, Chyna took the opportunity to whack Jarrett solidly with his own trademark move, the guitar. He fell to the mat, senseless. Chyna got the pin, and in that moment became the first woman ever to hold the Intercontinental belt

It had taken just under ten seconds to set the wrestling world on its ear.

Chyna—and Joanie—were thrilled. Her hands were held high, as they often are after winning matches, but this time one of those hands had a belt in it. The crowd went wild, knowing they were present at a new age of wrestling entertainment.

Chyna had entered the arena a contender. But she left it a champion. She also left behind her one of the messiest rings in wrestling history. Strangely, she left with more than just the belt. She took Miss Kitty with her.

The title bout between Stone Cold Steve Austin and Triple H later that night, in which Triple H retained the belt, was certainly thrilling, but it paled in comparison to Chyna's achievement. Because she was one step further down that road to holding the heavyweight belt herself.

There is no doubt in the minds of most wrestling aficionados that someday she will own it.

# CHAPTER 12

# HERE, KITTY, KITTY

Two roads diverged in the wrestling world, and fate decided that Triple H would walk down one, and Chyna the other. The success of the new WWF storylines indicated that they should separate onstage for a while, and so Chyna needed a new partner.

It all began when Vince McMahon's daughter Stephanie was due to marry Test. Triple H, determined to transform himself into the WWF's biggest heel, needed to make sure that did not happen. On the day the wedding was to take place before a packed arena and a national television audience, the ring was adorned with flowers and happy family members. But that happiness came to an end when Triple H interrupted the proceedings by forcing the celebrants to watch an unsettling film. In it, Triple H was shown pulling up to a drive-through Las Vegas wedding chapel in a convertible with an unconscious Stephanie McMahon in the passenger seat. Caught on film was a fraudulent wedding being held after Helmsley connived to have Stephanie drugged at her own bachelorette party. While the officiator was distracted with paperwork during the ceremony, Helmsley turned his head and spoke in a high-pitched voice to pretend that Stephanie was taking willing part. Somehow, the owner of the wedding chapel was fooled, and issued a legitimate wedding certificate.

Triple H was now Vince McMahon's son-in-law. The wedding to Test was off.

And the Helmsley-McMahon era had begun.

Stephanie denied she was together with Triple H, and tried to convince Test that she'd had nothing to do with it. But she soon came around to the dark side and clung to her role as Mrs. Helmsley, where together they began wreaking havoc throughout the WWF.

Of course, the relationship between Laurer and Levesque continued unabated, but the demands of their roles as Chyna and Triple H demanded that they act otherwise.

But as long as this sensational subplot was going on, Chyna needed a new companion, and so Stacy Carter, who came into the WWF allied with Jeff Jarrett, started purring as Miss Kitty for

Chyna. The Ninth Wonder of the World had not only won a belt, she'd won a sidekick as well. And while Miss Kitty when she first appeared was not exactly a Chyna "mini-me," with her blond hair and silver jumpsuits, she soon became a new leather-clad Miss Kitty with jet-black hair who suddenly did seem like a petite version of Chyna.

Miss Kitty first made her debut on the August 23rd episode of *RAW Is War* that was filmed at Iowa State University. She appeared with Jeff Jarrett and Debra as Debra's assistant, and the two women were often subjected to the bizarre rages of the macho man whose trademark move was to bang them over the head with his guitar. These rages were intended essentially to prove to Chyna that Jarrett knew how to handle women and someday intended to handle her, but Chyna was not impressed. She showed him that, beyond the shadow of a doubt, when she took his belt away.

Who was this new face on the field? It turns out she was not so new after all. She was the girl-friend of frenetic ring announcer and former wrestling champion Jerry "the King" Lawler. Lawler, at six feet and 240 pounds, was the AWA and WCCW champion, after making his pro debut in 1970. Those unfamiliar with the ins and outs of the wrestling world will probably know him best for his role in the Milos Forman movie, *Man on the Moon*, where he played himself, re-creating his strange relationship with manic performance comedian Andy Kaufman.

Lawler also happens to be the person Joanie Laurer considers "a laugh a minute."

Lawler met Carter at a charity softball game that was being held near the King's Memphis, Tennessee, home. Carter had dropped by the game to cheer on a family friend, and soon found herself in a deep relationship with Lawler.

Lawler wanted their romance to be not only personal, but professional as well, and he asked her to join him on-camera, as his valet. She followed him from the USWA to the Power Pro Federation. The storylines she was asked to perform must have seemed odd to a newcomer to the field, just as it must have been strange for her to be in a romantic relationship with the King of the Ring while at the same time acting for the cameras as if a fellow wrestler were stalking her, but that's what makes for wrestling "entertainment." Now her role demanded that she come out from under Lawler's shadow.

The night after Chyna won the Intercontinental belt on No Mercy, she appeared on *Monday Night RAW* with Miss Kitty beside her. The innocent

blond had turned into the black-haired vixen. Stacy was soon transformed into Chyna's valet instead of Jarrett's, and it was a more forceful role for her. She now seems well on the way to a solo career of her own, as the Kat, the name she prefers. When one ring announcer persisted in calling her Miss Kitty instead of the Kat, Carter quickly made her preference known by giving the announcer a trouncing.

Why did she move so quickly from Jarrett to Chyna? The fact that Jarrett jumped ship to the WCW was not the only reason for Carter's quick transition. Carter admits now that she was fascinated not by Jarrett the man, but rather by the golden belt he wore about his waist. That Intercontinental belt was one she longed to someday own for herself.

"When he lost it to Chyna, I had no more use for Mr. Jeff Jarrett," she has said. "I followed the gold . . . and that was with Chyna."

Though Miss Kitty is paired with Chyna, she is not forthcoming about what she might have learned from other wrestlers in the WWF, preferring to keep mum and not get involved in any rivalries—though she is willing to say that she admires fellow wrestling femme Debra for her beauty, friendliness, and sex appeal.

Stacy's sexual attributes perhaps got a little

more exposure than she counted on when women's champion Jackie tore Stacy's top off. But Miss Kitty knows what it is she's selling, and she isn't shy about it. "We are in the world of sports entertainment, and sex sells. If you want to sell something, whether it is a can of beer, an automobile, or a wrestling event, it is certainly all right to use sex to sell it."

And she has used that sex appeal on a regular basis. After winning the WWF women's title on December 12, 1999, at Armageddon, she performed a Brandy Chastain, and like that captain of the women's soccer team, stripped off her shirt—only she didn't stop there, but lifted her bra as well. WWF personnel quickly covered her up.

Miss Kitty is one of the few Americans lucky enough to visit a home even more awe-inspiring than the palatial McMahon mansion. On November 1, 1999, she was invited, along with *New York Times* bestselling author Mick Foley (aka Mankind and Cactus Jack) and Lawler to pay a visit to 1600 Pennsylvania Avenue for a tour of the Oval Office. Who knows if Miss Kitty has political aspirations? Even though Lawler has stated that "the White House is no place for a King," we might soon see another wrestler in politics.

After all, she was almost a first lady herself. Boyfriend Jerry Lawler ran for mayor of Memphis recently, and finished third with 11.7 percent of the votes, running against the incumbent and the City Council chairman. Considering his opponents, it was a respectable showing. And who knows, he might try again soon, putting another wrestling figure beside Jesse Ventura on the political map.

# CHAPTER 13

# THE FUTURE

When Joanie Laurer transformed herself from an uncertain teenager into Chyna, the Ninth Wonder of the World, she became many things, not all of them expected. If life went as she had planned and hoped from the beginning, she knew that she would have money and fame without limit. But it is doubtful she could have foreseen that she would not only become a celebrity, but she would also be taken up as a role model and a feminist icon. We expect wrestling to be entertaining, not inspirational. How refreshing that Joanie Laurer was able to surprise us all by doing both!

The corporate world has its infamous glass ceiling, and though this woman warrior went in for the Federation instead of the corporation, Joanie Laurer has burst all expectations in her own way, by ripping through wrestling's canvas ceiling.

On *National Enquirer* TV, she declared to the world, "I finally reached a point where I'm really happy in my life." And why shouldn't she be?

She has made herself the CEO of her own life.

No one would have predicted that Joanie would have come so far in such a short period of time. Those who knew her first saw the potential there, but with so many roadblocks along the way, foreseeing such a future was unimaginable. "I never expected it would be that fast," said Dr. Michael Lano, when asked whether he would have been willing to place a bet on her speedy success. "She had a real aptitude and eagerness and all of that, but I thought it would be six or seven years. They put her on TV, and that's her shot, and she ran with it so quickly, but no one could have ever predicted. None of us who ever met her or knew her would have guessed that this would happen. She's so lucky it didn't happen in some other organization. WWF knows how to market their stars and get them over in a hurry. When she got plucked for that role, she was big instantly. It was good that she was part of that team of talented current young minds of wrestling, like Shawn Michaels and Hunter and Scott Hall and Kevin Nash—what was known as the Clique—and she was the female part of it. It was sort of like the old Sinatra Rat Pack. The

most talented wrestlers and talented young minds, and the marketing genius of Vince McMahon. She got her shots. She was lucky, and it just really blossomed really quickly."

She is a strong woman, and has never been forced where she didn't want to go. These days, while lawsuits seem more prevalent among women wrestlers than figure four leglocks, Joanie Laurer has avoided that route. She has turned down storylines that she felt unsuitable for her personality, and her advice to other women wrestlers who are having issues with shameful storylines is to follow Nancy Reagan's advice and "Just say no!"

"There's never been another Chyna," Joanie recently told Jay Leno. "It's just worked out wonderfully. I'm this empowered woman who kicks guys in the nuts for a living."

She has proven what no female wrestler has proven before—that a woman can be athletic and strong and sexy and beautiful all at the same time, while not sacrificing one facet of her life for any of the others. And now that she's shown the wrestling world's toughest customers that she can handle them, Jane Fonda and Richard Simmons had better look out. Her exercise video will have hit the stores by the time this book comes out, creating a new generation of women who will use

Joanie's rules to mold their own lives. "There's not another one of me," she told MTV's *Timeout*, "and I hope there are in the future." Her video might be her first step in the master plan for world domination..

Joanie has indicated that her favorite awards show is the *American Music Awards*, but she has been making quite a splash lately in the audience of many different such shows, included the Oscars, the Emmys and the American Comedy Awards. She is often seen wearing striking outfits that have been specially created to fit the monument of her body, some so tight-fitting as to require the casting of her torso for their design. She once made it to the top of Mr. Blackwell's famed Worst Dressed List for one such outfit, but she wears that like a badge of honor.

But as far as awards shows go, she'd better keep the mantle ready for an Emmy, because she recently appeared on the USA Network show *Pacific Blue*, which airs following *Sunday Night Heat*. She followed Triple H onto that show, and Hunter Hearst Helmsley's appearance got the show its highest ratings to date, so we wait to see what Nielsen thinks of Chyna. Her role is that of a jewel thief named Tonya Sweet who, after her arrest, continues to beat up on the male police officers.

"It's fun to do something a little bit different,"

she has said. "It's kind of neat to be able to do some acting outside of what we do. I love what I do, but I would certainly love to expand and do other things and make myself as big a star as I could possibly be."

She is also soon to make a guest-star appearance on *Third Rock from the Sun*. Apparently, the alien character of Sally, played by the statuesque Kristen Johnson, is to battle it out with Chyna.

And there is surely more screen action to come, what with her aspirations to take her character to the next level. "Chyna should be her own character in a TV series," she said recently on *National Enquirer* TV. "I think Chyna should be the next female Terminator. She should be Wonder Woman 2000."

But Michael Lano assures us that unlike other ring personalities, Joanie is not about to turn her back on wrestling. "TV is not her main thing," he said recently, "as it was with Sable or some of these people who just want to use wrestling as a stepping-stone to get into acting. She loves wrestling. It's in her blood. She grew up watching it. At least from my standpoint, I think it's her first love. So it's not a real thought-out goal. If these extracurricular movie and TV things happen, so be it. WWF has some proposed movie deals, and she would be a big part of that if they were to occur."

But there are many other worlds still to conquer, more stereotypes left to attack. Vince McMahon, owner of the WWF, has just announced that he is starting a professional football league—called the XFL (the "X" standing for "exciting and exhilarating" according to the owner)—with teams in Washington, D.C., New York, San Francisco, Los Angeles, Miami, Orlando, and several other major cities. He promises that this will be a true sport and not scripted entertainment. McMahon's stated purpose is to bring back individuality to the sport of football, even as its more mainstream counterpart is banning the sort of triumphant displays that are the very core of wrestling. McMahon took a chance on Chyna before to break down barriers. Is there any chance that Chyna will do what many women athletes have wanted to do for so long, and break through to playing pro football? If any female can do it, Joanie Laurer is the one.

Chyna and football fans are holding their collective breaths.

Captain Lou Albano, the legendary wrestling manager who helped marry wrestling to rock when he appeared in Cyndi Lauper's music video of "Girls Just Want to Have Fun," commented

about Chyna's future in the pages of *WOW* magazine. "She is right up there with the big boys," he said, "working her butt off to entertain the public and bring them an exciting product to watch. I don't think we've seen everything she has to offer. Watch for her in the future to do even more."

What Joanie Laurer hopes that more will be is obviously the Heavyweight Championship belt. Lano, a ring observer for over three decades, thinks she very well might get her chance. "You never would have thought that she would have gotten the Intercontinental [shot], that was sort of a reward from the company for her loyalty, more than anything else. It wouldn't surprise me at all. No one ever said it's a man's heavyweight belt."

But new opponents wait around every corner, even after her recent triumphs over the likes of Val Venis and Road Dogg. Debra, famous for her puppies, plans on improving her wrestling abilities, and even though Steve Austin's fiancée has helped Chyna overcome obstacles in the past, the Ninth Wonder of the World is her likeliest future target. "I'm still training, trying to hone my wrestling skills. Those little girls in the WWF won't be able to survive once I become a lethal fighting machine." Whenever Debra is ready, Chyna will be there.

"No matter what they do," Lano says, "pair her with Jerry Lawler's girlfriend Kitty, whatever they do, she has this great rapport and the audience goes nuts for her. She's well-liked in the dressing room, so she was sort of a gift. She just clicked with audiences and magazines somehow. And the boys definitely have respect."

"I've earned respect," she told a rowdy chat room group via *MegaStar* in the U.K., "and those who protested the most at the start are now my biggest supporters."

She has said that given the chance to live her life over again, she wouldn't have done anything differently. And for that, her millions of fans are glad. Chyna has stated that the best advice she ever gave or heard was, "Ask and you shall receive." What can we do after hearing that except to say, "Chyna—more!"

Chyna is the new face of wrestling, and the world had better get used to it.

# DO YOU KNOW YOUR CHYNA?

Now that you've read this book, you should be an expert on the Ninth Wonder of the World. Below are twenty-five trivia quiz questions to determine just how much of a Chynamaniac you really are. Answer the following questions, then rate yourself on your Chyna knowledge.

1: Joanie Laurer has transformed herself into Chyna, the Ninth Wonder of the World. Who was considered the Eighth Wonder of the World?
a) Hulk Hogan
b) Gorgeous George
c) The Fabulous Moolah
d) Andre the Giant

2: As a child, what was Joanie Laurer's favorite book?

a) *Winnie the Pooh*

b) *Stanley the Steamshovel*

c) *The Little Engine that Could*

d) The Berenstain Bears


3: Walter "Killer" Kowalski's training camp, which turned out both Chyna and Triple H, is located in which state:

a) Rhode Island

b) California

c) Texas

d) Massachusetts


4: When Joanie was growing up watching wrestling, who was not one of her three favorite superstars?

a) Captain Lou Albano

b) Killer Kowalski

c) Gorgeous George

d) Bruno Samartino

5: Joanie Laurer received the wrestling training that would eventually turn her into Chyna from:

a) Bruno Samartino
b) Gorilla Monsoon
c) Hulk Hogan
d) Killer Kowalski

6: When Triple H and Chyna were touring Europe, in which country did they fall in love?

a) Spain
b) Germany
c) France
d) Italy

7: Who is Joanie Laurer's favorite actor?

a) Tom Hanks
b) Brad Pitt
c) Antonio Banderas
d) Arnold Schwarzenegger

8: When the readers of *Rampage* magazine were asked to name the toughest woman wrestler, Chyna received what percentage of the vote?

a) 100 percent
b) 90 percent
c) 80 percent
d) 70 percent

9: At the University of Tampa, Joanie Laurer majored in:
a) Spanish Literature
b) Political Science
c) Sports Medicine
d) Media and Communications

10: Who is Joanie's favorite singer?
a) Billy Joel
b) Frank Sinatra
c) Bruce Springsteen
d) Barbra Streisand

11: Joanie Laurer helped create her Chyna character with advice from Triple H and which other wrestler?
a) Shawn Michaels
b) Badd Ass Billy Gunn
c) Scott Hall
d) Bret Hart

12: Chyna's debut feud was with which wrestling opponent of Triple H?
a) Razor Ramon
b) The Rock

c) Stone Cold Steve Austin
d) Goldust

13: Chyna's favorite food is:
a) Pizza
b) Chicken
c) Steak
d) Ice Cream

14: When Chyna first appeared on TV, she took on the role of:
a) Valet
b) Bodyguard
c) Fan
d) Manager

15: During her career, which of the following wrestlers has she not been partnered with:
a) Kane
b) Triple H
c) Miss Kitty
d) Gangrel

16: When Chyna became the first woman to ever compete in the Royal Rumble in 1999, who eliminated her from the ring?
a) Triple H
b) The Big Show
c) Stone Cold Steve Austin
d) Kane

17:When she was allowed to enter the King of the Ring competition, Chyna faced off against which fellow wrestler?
a) X-Pac
b) Kane
c) Triple H
d) Sexual Chocolate

18: Whom did Chyna help win the European Championship title belt?
a) Road Dogg Jesse James
b) Badd Ass Billy Gunn
c) The British Bulldog
d) Shane McMahon

19: Which wrestling personality became so enamored of Chyna that he wrote her unwanted love poetry?
a) X-Pac
b) Mark Henry
c) Triple H
d) Vince McMahon

20: Chyna faced off against Triple H in a tag-team match on which national holiday?
a) Valentine's Day
b) Christmas
c) The Fourth of July
d) Labor Day

21: To win the Intercontinental Championship belt, Chyna delivered the finishing blow with which weapon?
a) A guitar
b) A kitchen sink
c) The Intercontinental belt itself
d) A trash can

22: Which slot did Chyna occupy at the Royal Rumble?
a) 15
b) 30
c) 2
d) 29

23: Who is Chyna's favorite athlete?
a) Muhammad Ali
b) Cal Ripken, Jr.
c) Mike Tyson
d) Joe DiMaggio

24: Chyna became the Intercontinental Champion by defeating which arrogant wrestler at the No Mercy pay-per-view event?
a) X-Pac
b) Jeff Jarrett
c) Road Dogg Jesse James
d) Chris Jericho

25: After Chyna had a falling out with Triple H, with which wrestler did she form an alliance?

a) Badd Ass Billy Gunn
b) Ken Shamrock
c) The Rock
d) Kane

Answers

1-D, 2-A, 3-D, 4-C, 5-D, 6-B, 7-D, 8-C, 9-A, 10-B, 11-A, 12-D, 13-B, 14-C, 15-D, 16-C, 17-A, 18-D, 19-B, 20-A, 21-A, 22-B, 23-C, 24-B, 25-D

If you got 25 correct: Congratulations! You're qualified to run the WWF!

If you got 20 correct: Good for you! Perhaps you should send your résumé to the WWF and take over Jerry "the King" Lawler's job.

If you got 15 correct: It's time you watched a few more pay-per-views.

If you got 10 correct: Too bad. Try staying home Monday nights more often.

If you got fewer than 5 correct: Are you sure that you've ever seen a wrestling match?

# TEXAS RATTLESNAKE

The unfiltered, completely unauthorized
story of
Steve "Stone Cold" Austin

## STEVE EDELMAN

TOTALLY UNAUTHORIZED, UNCENSORED,
AND RAW!

Grab hold of the real story of Steve Austin and his
meteoric rise to the top in today's hottest and wildest
entertainment. With his bold take-no-prisoners style,
this bullet-headed boss of the ring demands respect—
and gets it every time. From ECW to WCW and
WWF, Steve Austin delivers the goods, leaving his
dazed opponents stone cold!

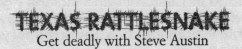

Get deadly with Steve Austin

Available at bookstores everywhere.
Published by Ballantine Books.

# PERFECT HARMONY
## The Faith Hill & Tim McGraw Story

## Scott Gray

Faith Hill and Tim McGraw are two of the hottest stars in country music. *Perfect Harmony* is a dazzling tribute to their inspiring story.

As a child in a small Mississippi town, Faith dreamed of someday making it big in Nashville. Tim grew up riding horses and playing baseball in rural Louisiana. Since meeting and falling in love on their Spontaneous Combustion tour in 1996, Faith and Tim have become known in Nashville as the new Mr. and Mrs. Country Music. As husband and wife, they've created a romance for the ages and a model marriage that includes two beautiful daughters.

Available at bookstores everywhere.
Published by Ballantine Books.

# Two is better than one!

## *COUNTRY'S GREATEST DUO*
## The Brooks & Dunn Story

*by*

## Jo Sgammato

Just mention foot-stomping honky tonk tunes, rich ballads, stylish videos, and an awesome stage show and people *know* you're talking about Brooks & Dunn. Here is the exciting story of a couple of guys at the top of their form: family men who love to make music, race cars, and thrill fans of all ages and musical tastes.

### *COUNTRY'S GREATEST DUO*
### The Brooks & Dunn Story
#### by Jo Sgammato

Published by Ballantine Books.
Available in bookstores everywhere.

*Read on . . .*
*More Country from Ballantine!*

# *KEEPIN' IT COUNTRY*
# The George Strait Story

*by*

# Jo Sgammato

*Keepin' It Country* explores what America loves so much about George Strait: the tremendous talent he generously shares while keeping his own life private, his authentic country life and spirit, and his renown as a true gentleman whose career is the bridge between the past and the future of country music.

Available in bookstores everywhere
or call 1-800-793-2665
with your credit card.

*The Dazzling Rise of
a Young Country Star*

**DREAM
COME
TRUE**

# THE LeANN RIMES STORY
by
Jo Sgammato

Who is this singer with the incredible voice, the youngest artist ever nominated for a Country Music Association Award, and winner of a Grammy Award for Best New Artist? Find out all this and more in this heartwarming story, complete with four pages of color photos!

Published by Ballantine Books.
Available at your local bookstore.

# A PIRATE LOOKS
## AT FIFTY
## by Jimmy Buffett

For the millions of fans of Jimmy Buffett's music as well as his bestselling books, here is the ultimate Jimmy Buffett philosophy on life and how to live it. As hard as it is to believe, the irrepressible Jimmy Buffett has hit the half-century mark, and in *A Pirate Looks at Fifty* he brings us along on the remarkable journey he took through the Southern Hemisphere to celebrate his landmark birthday.

For Parrotheads, armchair adventurers, and anyone who appreciates a good yarn and a hearty laugh, here is the ultimate backstage pass—you'll read the kind of stories Jimmy usually reserves for his closest friends, and you'll see a wonderful, wacky life through the eyes of the man who's lived it. *A Pirate Looks at Fifty* is a breath of fresh air and an ingenious manual for getting to fifty . . . and beyond.

Published by Fawcett Books.
Available in bookstores everywhere.

# Peter Bogdanovich's Movie of the Week

## 52 Classic Films for One Full Year

Director, producer, screenwriter, author, actor, and film critic, Peter Bogdanovich knows movies. Now, in this unique new book, he shares his passion with a connoisseur's insight and delight by inviting the reader to join him for a year at the movies—fifty-two weeks, fifty-two films, fifty-two reasons to watch.

With recommendations specific to the seasons and holidays—from sparkling comedies, timeless musicals, landmark foreign films, and powerful dramas and thrillers to legendary masterpieces and neglected treasures—Bogdanovich's eclectic cinematic calendar of classics, each available on video, each accompanied by an illuminating essay, and each followed by a list of tie-in recommendations, makes the perfect date for movie lovers every week of the year.

Published as a Ballantine trade paperback.
Available in a bookstore near you.